GLOBAL GEOGRAPHY

Learning through Development
Education at Key Stage 3

Reproduced from *Thin Black Lines,* DEC (Birmingham)

GLOBAL GEOGRAPHY

*Learning through Development
Education at Key Stage 3*

Produced by the Geographical Association in partnership with DEC (Birmingham)

EDITORS

Roger Robinson
Development Education Centre and School of Education, University of Birmingham

Jeff Serf
University of Wolverhampton

AUTHORS

Lucy Kirkham
Bridgnorth Endowed School, Shropshire

Roger Robinson
DEC and School of Education, University of Birmingham

Jeff Serf
University of Wolverhampton

Diane Swift
Staffordshire LEA

CONTRIBUTORS

Maureen Barwell
Cardinal Newman RC School, Birmingham

Clare Dabner
Hillcrest School, Birmingham

Lisa James
Cockshut Hill School, Birmingham

Shaun Lammond
Cardinal Wiseman RC School, Birmingham

Tim Thomas
Archbishop Illsley RC School, Birmingham

THE GEOGRAPHICAL ASSOCIATION

DEC (BIRMINGHAM)

Acknowledgements

Staff of DEC (Birmingham): Scott Sinclair, Catherine McFarlane, Fransisco Salazar, Ina Clason, Rachel Hayhow, Judy Lingard, Julie Simmonds.

The materials in this publication include ideas and resources developed by teachers in projects organised by Teachers in Development Education (TIDE) in the DEC (Birmingham). Specifically, we would like to acknowledge the following:

The 'Themework' project co-ordinated by Catherine McFarlane, and including Kate Culling, Celia Hargrave, Jackie Hughes, Jan Harris and Liz Ward.

The Development Compass Rose project co-ordinated by Scott Sinclair, Catherine McFarlane and Andrew Simons, and including Lorraine Anderson, Teresa Freeman, Larissa Gordon, Fiaz Hussain, Judith Richards and Linda Surga.

The DEC Geography programme:

The Gambia/Senegal study visit co-ordinated by Scott Sinclair and Roger Robinson, and including Jon Bruton, Ken Ellis, Kelvyn Davies, Keith King, Laurence Kimpton, John Kyte, Catherine McFarlane, Jeff Serf and Joyce Serf.

The 'Developing Geography' group co-ordinated by Jeff Serf and Scott Sinclair, and including Paul Archer, Maureen Barwell, Jon Bruton, Ken Ellis, John Hopkin, Leszek Iwaskow, Keith King, Veronica Lane, Roger Robinson, David Stanton, Diane Swift, Wayne Thomas and Nick Webster.

The Geography Modular Syllabus project co-ordinated by Scott Sinclair and including Roger Carter, Roger Robinson and Diane Swift.

The Ghana study visit co-ordinated by Jeff Serf and Roger Robinson and including Richard Beattie, William Elgar, Lucy Kirkham, Amanda Nicoll and Tim Thomas.

The Ghana Teachers project co-ordinated by Vivian Campbell and Kwesi Hutchful in Ghana with the support of Jeff Serf and Scott Sinclair and including many members of the Ghanaian Geographical Association.

The Birmingham issues project co-ordinated by Roger Robinson, Graham Butt and Ruth Tetlow, and including Nicola Arber, Maureen Barwell, Karen Broadbent, Claire Dabner, Lisa James, Jan Payne, Jeff Serf, Tim Thomas, Barrie Clark, Maura Clemson and Steve Thomas.

The Just Understanding Project:

'Beyond the backyard' team co-ordinated by Roger Robinson and including John Berry, Hazel Bloxham, Graham Butt, Ruth Hand, David Ilderton, Sandra Johnson, David Jones, Rachael Kemp, Linda Kent, Timothy Kilbride, Keith King, Ruth Miles, Rose Nsiah, Jeff Serf, Lesley Smith, David Stanton and Diane Swift.

The Taiwan study visit co-ordinated by Roger Robinson and including John Berry, Sandra Johnson, Rachael Kemp, Timothy Kilbride, Keith King and David Stanton.

ISBN 1 899085 29 7
The views expressed in this publication are those of the authors and do not necessarily represent those of the Geographical Association.

Published by the Geographical Association,
343 Fulwood Road, Sheffield S10 3BP.

The Geographical Association is a registered charity: no. 313129.

Design: Ledgard Jepson Ltd
Printed in England by Butler & Tanner

Contents

Development Education Centre (Birmingham)

DEC (Birmingham) is a small independent organisation working in partnership with teachers to bring a global dimension and a development perspective to the curriculum.

DEC has a policy of teacher involvement in all aspects of its work and in the management of DEC. TIDE (Teachers in Development Education) is a network designed to improve communication with people interested in the work of the Centre. Membership is available for individuals or schools.

**Development Education Centre,
Gillett Centre, 998 Bristol Road,
Selly Oak, Birmingham B29 6LE**

The Geographical Association

The Geographical Association is the national subject-teaching organisation for geography. Founded in 1893, it has over 11,000 members and local branches all over England, Wales and Northern Ireland. Nationally, hundreds of teachers contribute to the objectives of the Association through section committees, working groups and working parties.

Through its services to members — journals and publications, an Annual Conference, regional conferences, local branches — the GA provides curriculum support for teachers at all levels, extending and safeguarding geography's contribution to education.

**The Geographical Association,
343 Fulwood Road, Sheffield S10 3BP**

Preface

This handbook is the result of a collaboration between the Development Education Centre (Birmingham) and the Geographical Association. It has been written by practising teachers in secondary and tertiary education who have worked with the DEC in teachers' creative groups for several years and who in many cases have participated in DEC study visits abroad.

The book moves along a line from theory to practice. It is written to be used as a handbook open on the desk, or kept as an accessible resource in the geography storeroom. We hope it will be a stimulus and support for planning and teaching, as well as a practical guide for teacher and pupil activities.

Chapters 1 and 2 provide an overview of geography, development and development education.

Chapters 3 to 7 discuss teaching methods and the use of resources. They offer ideas for teachers, working singly or together, to plan and prepare schemes and lessons.

Chapters 8 and 9 are written by teachers who draw from their recent classroom experience of teaching about development through enquiry. Chapter 8 discusses the planning and implementation of a series of lessons on key stage 3 Country 'B', using Ghana as the subject. Chapter 9 provides a variety of key stage 3 lessons from different schools that exemplify some of the ideas in the handbook.

Chapter 10 references the work to the official curriculum documents.

Finally, a resource **appendix** recommends some of the classroom resources available.

Two companion guides should be mentioned:

1 The *International Charter on Geographical Education* is endorsed by the International Geographical Union and commended by the GA. It was reprinted in the April 1995 *Teaching Geography*. It supports many principles that underpin a development education approach. It emphasises enquiry and communication among the skills to be contributed by geography to pupils' education. It recommends an issue based approach at a variety of scales. It states that studying geography should be conducive to the development of attitudes and values that include a commitment to human rights and a willingness to participate privately and publicly to improve the quality of life.

2 *Global Perspectives in the National Curriculum: Guidance for Key Stage 3 — Geography* (DEA 1996) is a very useful 12-page publication. It provides a detailed account of how development education matches with the National Curriculum Geography Orders, and recommends resources for planning and teaching in that context.

The authors of **Global Geography** hope that by sharing their experience of geography and development education they will encourage other teachers to experiment with the ideas and practical suggestions. We hope that this handbook will not only reinforce the work of the 'converted' but also be useful to all geography students and teachers.

The divided world — terminology
In this handbook we have used a variety of names for the part of the world where over 75% of the world's people live but use less than 25% of the world's resources.
We have used **Third World**, not in a hierarchical sense, but in the sense of a third power to balance the worlds of capitalism and communism. Now that the communist world has disintegrated, the original sense may be more obscure.
We have used the **South** as the Brandt Report accepted it, even though it is geographically inaccurate.
We have used the **Developing World** because it is positive, even though it implies that the rest of the world is not developing!
We have not used the Undeveloped World, because it implies that nothing has happened there, and because its opposite (the Developed World) denies that development is taking place elsewhere.
We have not used the Underdeveloped World, because it assumes just one particular view of world history.
We have not used the World Bank/United Nations classification of ELDCs — Economically Less Developed Countries — because of its total reliance on GDP as a criterion.
We have tended to refer to the part of the world with 25% of the people using 75% of the resources as the 'rich, industrialised nations'.
There are weaknesses and strengths in all these names, and they are politically important.

Chapter 1:
Development Education
and Geography

Introduction

Following the Dearing Review of the National Curriculum, teachers have been promised a respite after the period of frenetic change of the late 1980s and early 1990s. While this is to be welcomed, it is also to be exploited. Geography teachers need to reflect on the lessons of the past few years, and consider what they and their subject can offer to children and young people.

Development education has a number of contributions to make to the debate about the role of geography in schools: these relate to how geography should be taught and to what content, topics and themes should be taught.

However, we cannot explore what development education has to offer unless we also explore what development education is:

> *Development education ... is fundamentally about a way of approaching things which will empower children to develop and express viewpoints and heighten their awareness of the ways they are linked to other people, and our planet both globally and locally.*

(Ange Grunsell, North London Oxfam Education Unit)

Development in the Geography National Curriculum

The topic of development featured on many syllabuses prior to the National Curriculum. However, the post-Dearing Order cites development as one of the key stage 3 themes, and its implications for key stages 1 and 2 cannot be ignored either.

What makes the Development theme particularly welcome is its recognition that development is not limited to the South but applies to all parts of the world. It is less parochial and Eurocentric than it may have appeared previously. The revised Order also supports an enquiry process for the whole geography curriculum and emphasises study at a variety of scales from local to global, and the interrelationships between them.

In attempting to exploit the period of relative stability promised after Dearing, geography teachers would do well to look at the potential of development education. Many teachers have already found it to be a fruitful area for ideas, approaches and perspectives with which to enrich the geography curriculum. The integration of development education will strengthen school geography and keep it centre-stage in the evolution of an education for future informed world citizenship.

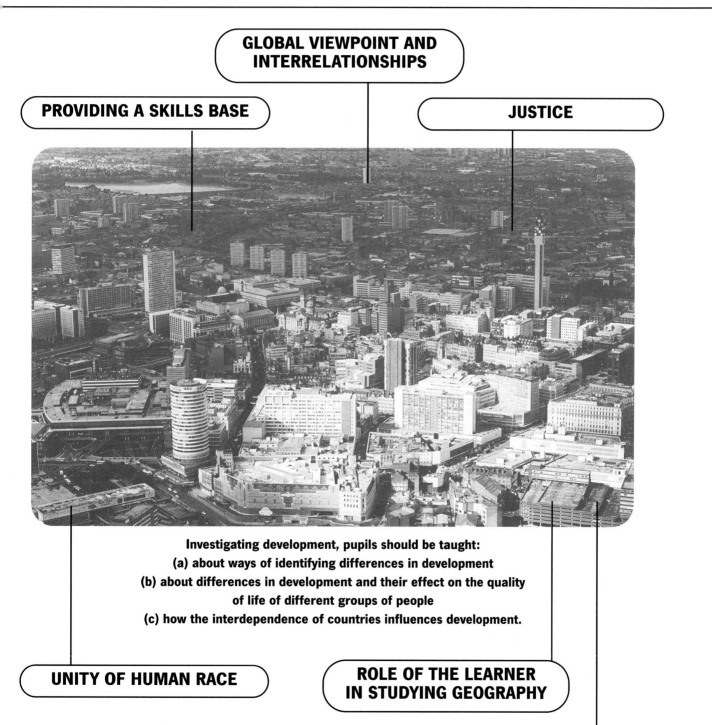

GLOBAL VIEWPOINT AND INTERRELATIONSHIPS

PROVIDING A SKILLS BASE

JUSTICE

Investigating development, pupils should be taught:
(a) about ways of identifying differences in development
(b) about differences in development and their effect on the quality
of life of different groups of people
(c) how the interdependence of countries influences development.

UNITY OF HUMAN RACE

**ROLE OF THE LEARNER
IN STUDYING GEOGRAPHY**

**ATTENTION TO THE
REAL WORLD**

The National Curriculum Development Theme

What is development education?

Development education explores development issues, global to local, in the context of justice. It is about participation in society, and emphasises skills and attitudes as well as knowledge. It aims to create understanding of development processes both here and in the wider world, and to help pupils recognise different perspectives.

It has been suggested that the diversity and looseness of development education are strengths, in that they have allowed its penetration into many areas of the curriculum. However, precisely because development education is holistic, it is often disregarded by subject specialists in secondary education. It is important to recognise what development education is and does, so that we can recognise what it has to offer.

Development education promotes an active-learning, pupil-centred teaching philosophy which calls for the use of debate and decision skills in geographical studies. This methodology, requiring freedom, individual value and democracy in the classroom, is an essential element of development education, but by no means is its only characteristic.

There are at least six areas where development education can either initiate or support those concerns that are central to geography in schools:

1 The global viewpoint and interrelationships

Situations anywhere in the world are the result of interrelationships of many kinds at many levels and scales. Areas that can be labelled 'the Third World' or 'the South' are not the only appropriate contexts for development education. To understand fully, say, the Heartlands Project in central Birmingham, or the Volta Project in Ghana, a global viewpoint is essential. Geography can look to development education for help in explaining these dimensions.

2 The unity of the human race

The focus on people in development education provides geography with an important antidote to endless images and information about things and landscapes, in which people appear only 'to give the scale'. The importance of people and their responsibility for the world is central to school geography. Understanding situations and issues around the world demands an understanding of people's actions and decisions, and at least a willingness to empathise with people in other places.

3 The role of the learner in the study of school geography

Human experience is central to the study of school geography. Development education provides an excellent means to recognise pupils' own experiences and to challenge them with new perspectives.

4 Justice

Social and economic human rights are high on the agenda for development education. It is simply unacceptable to assess explicitly pupils' beliefs and values (although we do it implicitly all the time). It is, however, very important to help pupils evaluate their own beliefs, attitudes and values, and understand how they use them to evaluate the world around them. To present an amoral physical and economic world where things 'just happen' and situations 'just exist' would be a disservice to the pupils. Development education can help teachers avoid this danger. Thus, geography continues to help pupils see how most situations are created and controlled by people who then have a responsibility for justice and human rights.

5 Providing a skills base

'Accept nothing at face value: question all assumptions' might be a motto for development education. To question effectively, to search for understanding of complex and continually changing issues, and to evaluate evidence are skills needed by all members of a true democracy. These skills cannot be taught in a didactic way: they have to be built up through practice — through talking, listening and debating. Pupils need to be confident of their ability to exercise such skills, and in doing so they will develop a sense of their own identity and value.

In giving this radical element to geography, development education owes much to Paulo Freire and Carl Rogers. If this element is missing from the geography classroom, once again we do a disservice to our pupils and to society.

6 Attention to the real world

All studies in development education need to be sited in the real world. Thus geography and development education once again have a common agenda. Controversial and complex topics such as sustainable development or differing life opportunities need a thoughtful approach in the classroom if they are to be made accessible to pupils. Development education provides the tools to do this.

Source: *TES,* 29.9.95

Development education in key stage 3 geography

1 The global viewpoint and interrelationships

Dearing's revised Order provides a structure to keep process, change and people at the centre of school geography, and an appreciation and analysis of interrelationships permeates the Programmes of Study. The linkages between scales, local through to global, the relationships between core and peripheral areas and between nations, and the interaction of social, political and environmental elements is essential to understanding people and places.

One tool that geographers can borrow from development education and make effective use of is the **Development Compass Rose.** In this, the cardinal points of the compass are replaced by four major dimensions or processes affecting the geography of places, while directions between the dimensions (e.g. SE) stimulate thoughts about some of the combined effects of social and economic factors.

The concept of 'local' needs to be redefined away from that of the immediate vicinity of the pupil. Everywhere is local to someone, and by placing a locality at the centre of the Development Compass Rose we can more easily consider the different processes operating on that locality and its people.

The Compass Rose activity can be extended to unravel links and relationships between different scales. Superimposing a concentric pattern onto the Rose can enable the initial responses to be classified into local, regional, national and global groups (see pages 44-45).

Natural
These are questions about the environment – energy, air, water, soil, living things, and their relationships to each other. These questions are about the 'built' as well as the 'natural' environment.

Who decides?
These are questions about power, who makes choices and decides what is to happen; who benefits and loses as a result of these decisions and at what cost?

Economic
These are questions about money, trading, aid and ownership.

Social
These are questions about people: their relationships, traditions and culture, and the way they live. They include questions abuot how, for example, gender, race, disability, class and age affect social relationships.

The Development Compass Rose

2 The unity of the human race

'Children can't empathise with a sack of cocoa beans, but they might be able to appreciate why the farmer grows them.' Human action is central to much of school geography, but many of our pupils have stereotyped images of people and places. To enable pupils to understand why people make certain decisions and act in certain ways, and to challenge the stereotypes we all hold, information about individuals is essential. By studying individuals, exploring aspects of their views, experiences, lifestyles and decision-making patterns, in the context of the wider social, economic and political scene, we make those people accessible to our pupils. Such cameos and life histories provide colourful case studies of people set against the background of their environment and experiences.

3 The role of the learner in studying geography

Geography has an advantage over many other school curriculum areas in that it can explore pupils' own experiences and their knowledge of the world. But how can we use this advantage? Development education can support a classroom environment that enables pupils to participate and take responsibility for their own learning and their own actions. Classroom knowledge can be opened up to include the pupils' own knowledge that they use outside the classroom. These two kinds of knowledge are often kept apart, and much of what is taught is not applied to subsequent experience. Knowledge relevant to the outside world will be regenerative, created, controlled and used by the learner. It is personal, and pupils' private geographies should be recognised, respected and fostered in our lessons. By using mental maps, role-plays and simulations, we should encourage pupils to exploit and refine their personal geographies.

4 Justice

People view the world from a variety of different starting points depending, for example, on where they have come from, their gender, age, ethnic or cultural background, or their economic situation. They make different judgements about what is going on.

Pupils must learn that there are different perspectives on a given issue if they are to appreciate that their view of the world is only one among many. Further, they need to evaluate events and situations against criteria that reflect not only their position — for example, how they will be influenced — but also how others will be affected. A full consideration of 'Who gains and who loses?' will allow pupils to explore an issue in a context that includes political, social and economic human rights. The use of Key Questions is one good way of doing this (see Chapter 4).

Source: **Who Runs the World** Christian Aid 1994

5 Providing a skills base

The issues that we and our pupils face are complex and continually changing. To deal with them, we need to help them develop the appropriate skills that are essential for collaborative and participatory work in school and for effective participation in society.

> Development education is about developing skills necessary for effective participation in the world:
> - skills of recognising one's own values and the influences upon them
> - skills of empathy with people in different situations and with different cultures
> - skills of acquiring information and being able to analyse it critically
> - skills of recognising the validity of different points of view
> - skills of forming one's own conclusions
> - skills of recognising the way one relates to the world
> - skills of recognising possibilities for future action.

6 Attention to the real world

The geography National Curriculum puts 'Place' in a central position for school geography. There have been criticisms that our pupils have been learning 'placeless' geography, and this may still be true in some instances. In selecting places to study, there is a danger of presenting a range of isolated case studies of exotic, biased and stereotypical images. If used effectively, the strategies and approaches offered by development education provide the means to avoid doing our pupils such a catastrophic disservice.

Geography contributes to development education too

The links between geography and development education are two-way — development education can contribute to geographical education, but the reverse is also true. The Geographical Association has described some of the contributions geography makes to pupils' general education, and all of them are relevant to development education (see panel).

Development education gains a great deal when it accepts the potential contribution of geography.

Geography's contributions to development education
World knowledge
International undertaking
Environmental awareness
Graphicacy

Extracts from the key stage 3 National Curriculum
Pupils should be given opportunities to:
- consider the issues that arise from people's interaction with their environments
- become aware of the global context within which places are set, how they are interdependent, and how they may be affected by processes operating at different scales, e.g. how a locality is affected by a regional economic policy or a world trade agreement.

Geographical skills
- identify geographical questions and issues and establish an appropriate sequence of investigation
- identify the evidence required and collect, record and present it
- analyse and evaluate the evidence, draw conclusions and communicate findings.

Pupils should be taught to:
- select and use secondary sources of evidence — photographs (including vertical and oblique aerial photographs), satellite images and other sources, e.g. census data, visits to school by representatives of local interest groups — to inform their studies.

For each of the two countries, pupils should be taught:
- about the ways in which the country may be judged to be more or less developed
- how the country is set within a global context and how it is interdependent with other countries.

Geography adds to development education
Spatial awareness and spatial skills
    — patterns, concepts, perception
    — mapping and map-reading
Analysis and synthesis of statistical data
Critical awareness of data sources
Attention to the scientific dimensions of environmental and economic issues
Rigour in analysis of situations

Chapter 2:
What is *Development?*

Development

Investigating development, pupils should be taught
a) about ways of identifying *differences in development*
b) about *differences in development and their effect on the quality of life of different groups of people*
c) how the *interdependence of countries* influences development.

From the *Geography National Curriculum*, 1995

In this chapter, we examine how these National Curriculum requirements can be taught.

a) Differences in development

That differences in development exist is obvious to our pupils; global media coverage exposes them to events and situations from around the world which often highlight differences in development. By concentrating on the spectacular, the unusual and the newsworthy, we are presented with images that reflect such characteristics, regardless of how commonplace they really are. The media often highlight the differences rather than the similarities between people and places, and also tend to provide trite, over-simplistic explanations of why these differences exist.

Unfortunately a common image is that of the drought-affected area, usually 'somewhere in Africa', with its barren landscape and miserable inhabitants. If we are to serve our pupils well, they should be taught that such events are not representative of the whole continent. Further, they must be taught to consider what factors have brought that situation about, and that it is not simply a case of too many people or not enough water.

Measuring development

In geography, we teach our pupils that we can measure development by using a number of indices. However, these indices mask the variation that exists within each country. Further, one can question the extent to which they really measure development. The limitations of statistics such as Gross National Product (GNP) per capita are widely recognised, and so various suggestions have

Country	GNP per capita 1993 (US$)	HDI ranking 1995	Life expectancy 1993 (years)	Under-5 mortality rate (per 1000 births)
Switzerland	35760	2	77.8	8
USA	24740	8	75.6	10
UK	18060	10	75.8	8
Ireland	13000	21	75.0	7
Greece	7390	25	77.3	10
Malaysia	3140	57	70.4	17
Georgia	580	66	73.0	28
Romania	1140	72	69.9	29
South Africa	2980	93	62.2	69
China	490	94	70.5	43
Jordan	1190	98	67.3	27
El Salvador	1320	112	65.2	60
Bolivia	760	113	60.5	114
Gabon	4960	114	52.9	154
Bangladesh	220	146	52.2	122
Mozambique	90	159	46.5	282

The Human Development Index (HDI) ranking — national differences in development

been made about composite indices: for example, the United Nations Development Programme's Human Development Index (HDI) is based upon life expectancy, educational attainment (adult literacy rate and mean years of schooling) and income (purchasing power expressed in parity dollars).

- Gender differences appear in the HDI: in all countries men do better than women in every socio-economic indicator except life expectancy.
- Like all indices of development, HDI has its limitations. It is political in that it was designed to focus attention on health and education, rather than on traditional economic features. It also highlights relative rather than absolute development, thus under-representing the progress of poorer countries.

Page 18 describes HDI and other international measures of development, and Chapter 5 suggests a teacher activity using these resources.

Ward	% unemployment	% permanently sick	% households with no car
Aston	33	15	73
Brandwood	12	10	42
Handsworth	29	13	59
Sparkbrook	33	16	69
Sutton Four Oaks	5	5	17
Yardley	13	11	43

Employment, health and wealth in six Birmingham wards
— local variations in development

Map of Birmingham showing wards
Source: **Birmingham City Council**

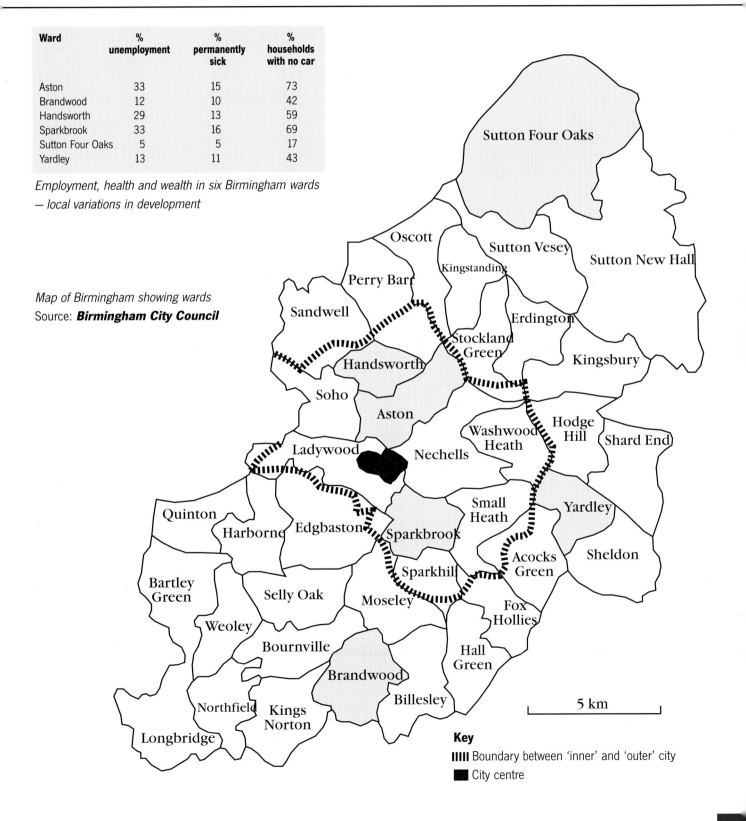

Key

|||| Boundary between 'inner' and 'outer' city

■ City centre

International measures of development

Gross National Product (GNP)
Gross Domestic Product (GDP)
Both measured in US dollars (US$)

Very similar measures
GDP measures the total output of goods and services produced by an economy, by both residents and non-residents, in one year.
GNP is the GDP plus income from abroad but minus payments to non-residents.

Human Development Index (HDI)

Measured as an index between 0.000 (a very low level of development) and 1.000 (the highest level of development at the moment).
Calculated from life expectancy, adult literacy, educational enrolment, educational attainment and Real GDP per capita .
Real GDP is discounted above about PPP$5000, assuming that income above this threshold is of progressively less use.

Real GDP

Measured in purchasing-power parity dollars (PPP$), GDP is adjusted to take into account the differences between the cost of living in the USA and in each country.
In India, for example, you can buy much more for a US dollar than you can in the USA.
This is a much more realistic measure of comparison than raw GDP.

Gender-related Development Index (GDI)

Measured as an index like HDI
Calculated on a similar basis to HDI, but taking into account the differences between women and men.

Comparing international measures of development

Ranking the world's countries for Real GDP, HDI and GDI provides a manageable set of statistical data for studying global patterns of development.

These lists are produced each year in the *Human Development Report.* Mapping the ranked countries in quintiles identifies spatial patterns. The comparison of ranks (also listed in the Human Development reports) identifies countries where HDI or GDI is better or worse than might be expected from their Real GDP. Mapping 'residuals' is a useful way to show these relationships. Work with world statistics goes hand in hand with practical atlas work and developing a world knowledge-base.

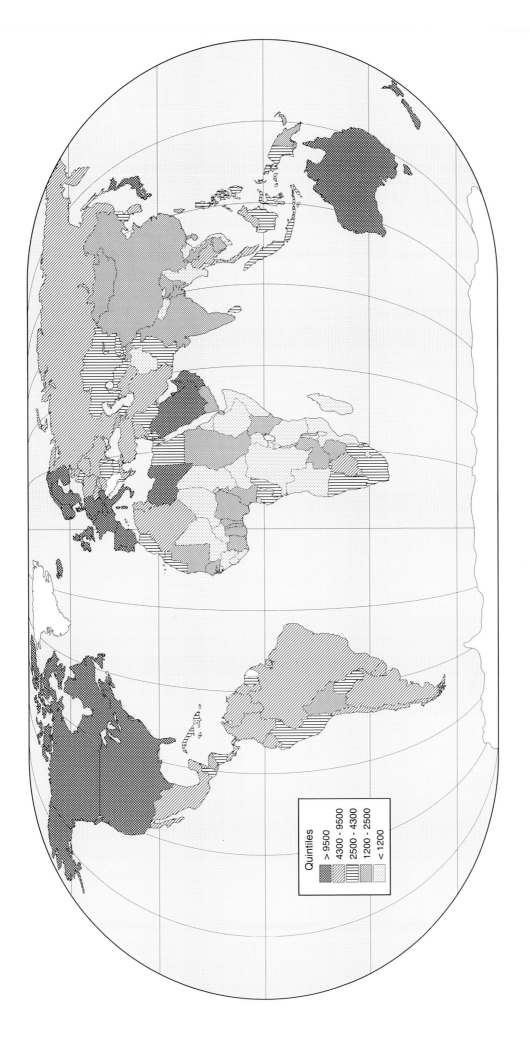

Quintiles	
> 9500	
4300 - 9500	
2500 - 4300	
1200 - 2500	
< 1200	

World map, mapped by quintiles (PPP$)

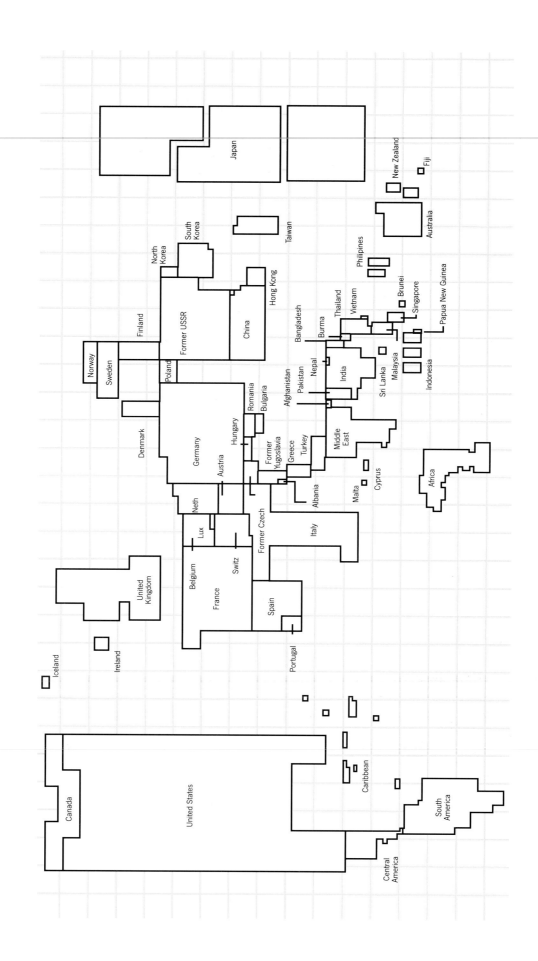

The distribution of world GNP

World map in which the size of each country is in proportion to its GNP (not GNP per capita!)

Source: *Human Development Report* 1995

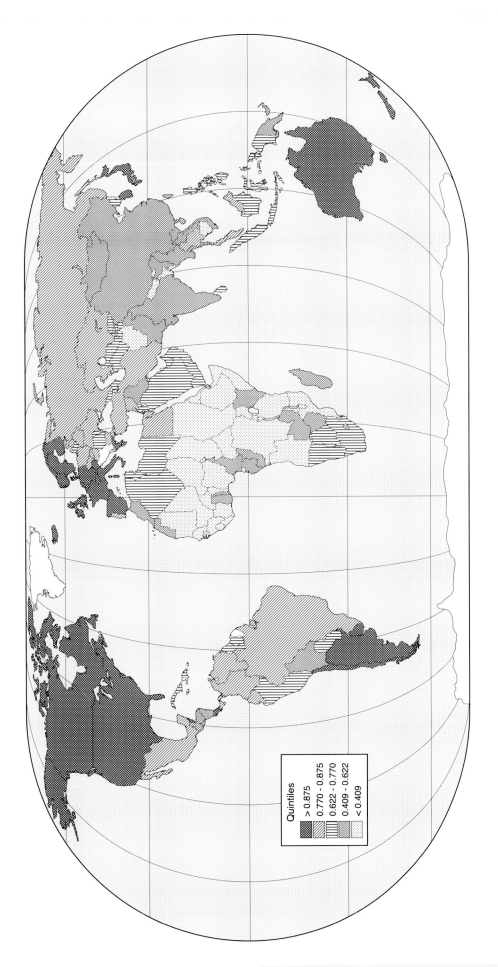

Quintiles
> 0.875
0.770 - 0.875
0.622 - 0.770
0.409 - 0.622
< 0.409

Note: Nine multinational enterprises (MNEs) (six Japanese and three from the United States) have annual sales of over US$100 000 million. Only 30 countries have a GNP of over US$100 000 million!

Human Development Index (HDI) 1992

Comparison of world rankings for Real GDP and HDI 1992

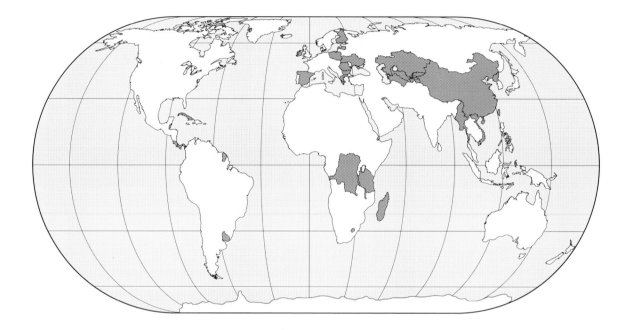

World map showing countries with HDI better than expected (a difference of 10 or more ranks)

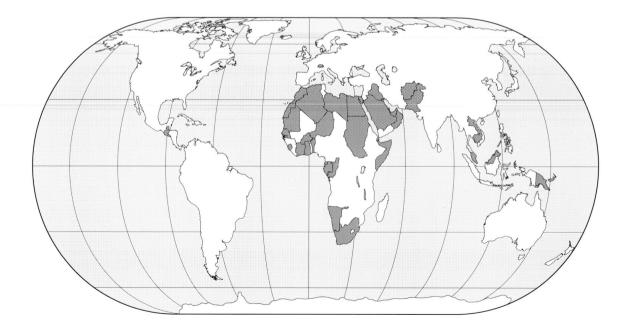

World map showing countries with HDI worse than expected
Source: *Human Development Report* 1995

Comparison of world rankings for HDI and GDI 1992

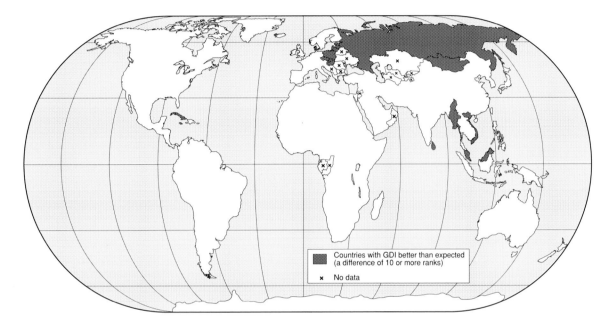

World map showing countries with GDI better than expected

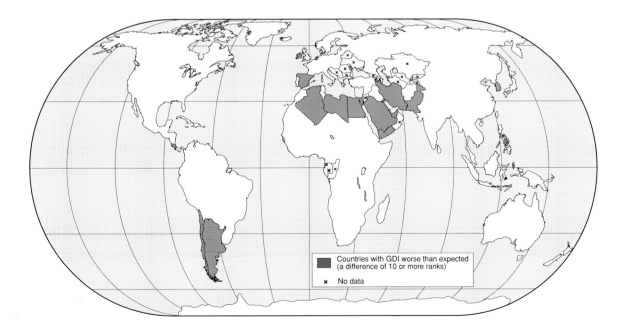

World map showing countries with GDI worse than expected
Source: *Human Development Report* 1995

Economic activities

Differences in economic development are often explored in geography lessons, but too often attention is directed at only traditional economic features that can be measured in money terms. To develop pupils' understanding of development, they also need access to information and ideas about the lives of real people, so that their perception is not limited by stunted images from official statistics and value-judgements based on the money economy.

One feature that should be addressed is the variation in economies and, in particular, the role of the informal economy. Here, *What are economic activities?* attempts to make the complex functioning of an economy accessible to pupils, while *A country's economic activity* gives a breakdown of a country's total production.

Teaching pupils to identify differences in development is not as straightforward as it may at first appear, especially if they are to be aware of what forces bring about the differences, and how they operate selectively within a given society.

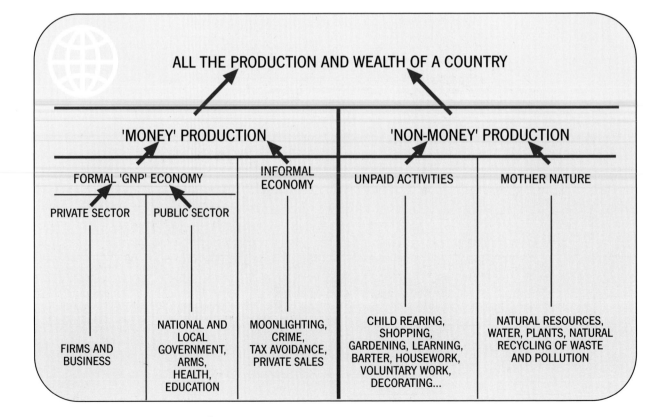

A country's economic activities

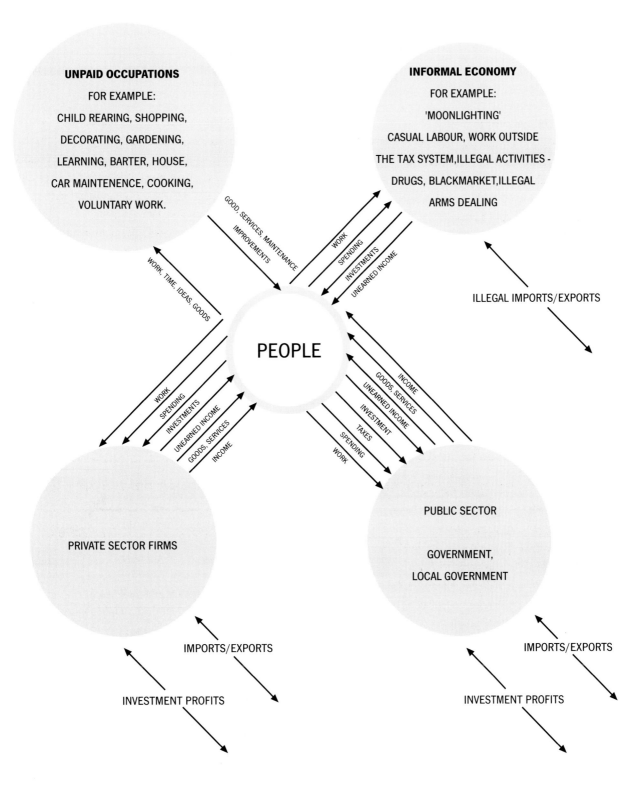

UNPAID OCCUPATIONS

FOR EXAMPLE:
CHILD REARING, SHOPPING,
DECORATING, GARDENING,
LEARNING, BARTER, HOUSE,
CAR MAINTENENCE, COOKING,
VOLUNTARY WORK.

INFORMAL ECONOMY

FOR EXAMPLE:
'MOONLIGHTING'
CASUAL LABOUR, WORK OUTSIDE
THE TAX SYSTEM,ILLEGAL ACTIVITIES -
DRUGS, BLACKMARKET,ILLEGAL
ARMS DEALING

GOOD, SERVICES, MAINTENANCE
IMPROVEMENTS

WORK
SPENDING
INVESTMENTS
UNEARNED INCOME

ILLEGAL IMPORTS/EXPORTS

WORK, TIME, IDEAS, GOODS

PEOPLE

INCOME
GOODS, SERVICES
UNEARNED INCOME
INVESTMENT
TAXES
SPENDING
WORK

WORK
SPENDING
INVESTMENTS
UNEARNED INCOME
GOODS, SERVICES
INCOME

PRIVATE SECTOR FIRMS

PUBLIC SECTOR

GOVERNMENT,
LOCAL GOVERNMENT

IMPORTS/EXPORTS

INVESTMENT PROFITS

IMPORTS/EXPORTS

INVESTMENT PROFITS

What are economic activities?

Myths of world hunger

'Nature is to blame'

Myth: Droughts and other events beyond human control cause famine.

Reality: Droughts, floods and other disasters happen to people who are already vulnerable. Drought is not a problem in itself. Vast areas of the United States are prone to drought but with irrigation can yield fruitful harvests. Even in sub-Saharan Africa, of 31 drought-affected countries in the early 1980s, only five have experienced famine. In each case — Mozambique, Angola, Sudan, Chad, Ethiopia — famine occurred in the context of war. Even in drought-affected regions, food is available to those with money. In blaming nature we also fail to recognise the human forces generating imbalances in nature e.g. overgrazing, monocropping, deforestation.

'There are too many mouths to feed'

Myth: There are too many people and not enough food to go round.

Reality: Because population growth and hunger can occur side by side, it is often thought that the first causes the second. In fact poverty causes both. The world produces enough grain alone to provide every human being with one-and-a-half times the necessary calories per day — if it were distributed equally. Over 40% of the world's grain supply is now fed to animals. Producing more food is not the solution to world hunger. Already global production is increasing faster than population. This myth distracts attention from the over-consumption of rich nations where 22% of the world's population consume more than 60% of the world's food.

'Corruption and ignorance are to blame'

Myth: This myth has two variations:
1 Third World leaders are corrupt and more concerned with lining their own pockets
2 They are ignorant and incapable of solving their own problems.

Reality: Each of the above statements is a cop-out and blames the victims. Corruption does happen in poor countries, but can we afford to point the finger? Look at the illegal receipts from EU agricultural funds.

'Moving our surpluses is the answer'

Myth: More food-aid and foreign assistance is needed.

Reality: There are many problems associated with food-aid, although it can provide short-term relief in time of famine. It may not reach the very poorest because of management and delivery problems. It tends to create dependence on imports and on food not produced locally. It can be used as a political lever by donor and recipient governments. It can destroy local farmers' markets and incentives to produce. A recent example was the disposal of EU beef surpluses at subsidised prices onto West African countries. With more than four million people in the Sahel depending upon cattle-rearing for their livelihood, this dumping of cheap beef had serious repercussions.

'A green revolution is needed'

Myth: More intensive farming and technology is the answer for hungry farmers.

Reality: It is true that new seeds and technology have undoubtedly increased the overall level of food production, and the amazing increase in world food-production should not be minimised. However they have failed to reduce the levels of vulnerability to hunger and malnutrition in Third World countries. Only rich farmers can afford to produce the high yields, only those with money can buy the produce.

from *Vocation for Justice*, Volume 9 Number 2 (Summer 1995)

Hunger - the real causes

Debt

The Third-World debt stands at about US$1,945,000 million. This debt burden is a major contribution to food shortages and famine, because countries are forced to use their best lands to earn cash by growing crops for export. Much of the best land in Ethiopia is devoted to growing coffee (80% of exports) and in Sudan to cotton (50% of exports). Similarly, in Somalia the best land is devoted to producing fruit, vegetables and cotton for export. During the famines in Ethiopia, Sudan and Somalia these countries were exporting food to earn foreign currency. Sub-Saharan African countries are together currently paying an average US$10 billion per annum in debt servicing. According to UNICEF the same amount would provide health and education services, safe water and other basic needs to every person on the continent.

The low status of women

In many countries inequality in provision of education, nutrition, and health services for women and girls is still a major cause of under-development. Women, although the producers of 80% of the world's food, are often the most vulnerable to food shortages and malnutrition. When food is scarce, women eat less and eat last. With the current squeeze on credit, women farmers face particular difficulties in gaining cash to purchase seeds, tools, fertilisers, etc. Under Structural Adjustment the push for export-led growth and cash crops means that women are working longer and harder to produce both crops for export and food for household consumption. Another key factor in women's inequality is that they are often denied educational opportunities. This has obvious implications for their capacity to break out of poverty.

Arms sales and wars

During 1993, 34 major armed conflicts were waged in 28 locations around the world. Not surprisingly most of these war zones are in the South. While global military spending has fallen in the 1990s due to the end of the Cold War, the latest estimates show current military spending by developing countries to be US$125 billion annually. Less than half this sum would be enough to provide all the basic needs of the population of those countries. Take the case of Pakistan. In 1992 the government ordered 40 Mirage 2000E fighters and three Tripartie aircraft from France. The cost of that one deal could have provided safe water for two years for all the 55 million Pakistanis who lack it, family-planning services for the estimated 20 million couples, essential medicines for the nearly 13 million people without access to health care, and basic education for the 12 million children not in primary school.

Unfair trade and low commodity prices

Unfair trade and the structure of global markets cost developing countries US$500 billion a year — 10 times what they receive in aid. Trade barriers directly discriminate against poor countries by stopping them exporting manufactured goods. Rich countries have increasingly protected their own economies while forcing poor countries to open up theirs. Even so, by 1990 56% of developing countries' exports were in manufacturing, often textiles. Most developing countries are, however, still trapped into selling commodities which have plummeted in value since the 1980s. Sale of primary products makes up 90% of the exports from African countries and 65% of those from Latin American countries. Between 1940 and 1990 world trade increased elevenfold, and yet the Third World, with 80% of the world's people, has still only 20% of its trade. Sub-Saharan Africa's trade share has fallen to a third of its 1960 level. One OECD estimate calculates Africa's losses at US$2.6 billion per annum as a result of the GATT.

b) Differences in development and their effect on the quality of life of different groups of people

Increasing awareness of environmental issues and the growth of green consumerism have brought the link between development and quality of life to the forefront of debate, and so into the classroom. *Agenda 21,* from the Rio Conference, is being treated seriously at both government and local levels. The need for a sustainable approach to the use of basic resources is an issue that is fundamental to the way in which development affects the quality of differing groups of people.

It is important that pupils are familiar with the concept of renewable and non-renewable resources. In the case of non-renewable resources such as coal and oil, a sustainable approach involves considering the needs of future generations and not over-exploiting the resources in the short term.

Renewable resources such as soil, timber, water or fish must be managed so that natural processes can replenish them. Failure to do so results in the renewable resources becoming non-renewable.

Sustainable development involves justice for future generations; it should also involve justice for the present generation. Justice will probably manifest itself in the interrelationships that exist between components of development, such as wealth, environment and population.

Activities can be designed to encourage pupils to consider the interaction of factors that may be at work. The pupils should also be stimulated to think about what action may be needed to ensure that all members of a society — their own local community, UK society or the global community — benefit from development.

- Core economic processes involve relatively high-technology, high-wage production, with high capital investment.
- Periphery processes are at the other end of the scale — relatively low-technology, low-wage production, with low capital investment.
- Both core and periphery processes can take place in one industry.
- One set of processes cannot exist without the other. The formation of capital and wealth at the core is made possible by the labour and resources of the periphery.
- Core regions tend to be affluent; peripheral regions tend to be poor and to have relatively high unemployment.

Why are economic core/periphery concepts so important to geography and development?

1 **Spatial form** — core and periphery can be recognised on maps

2 **Scale** — core and periphery patterns occur at all scales across the world.

3 **Process** — core and periphery models are not static: they change with time.

The concept of core and periphery

Core/periphery patterns

The divisions between local, regional, national and global are becoming increasingly blurred, especially in relation to decision-making. Decisions made in one locality may affect people and places across several continents. We can no longer assume, if we ever could, that developments in, say, Birmingham, result from decisions made in the UK or even Europe. The job prospects and quality of life for the inhabitants of a Sparkbrook housing estate are now just as likely to be affected by decisions made in Taiwan as by those made in the town hall.

The idea of 'core' and 'periphery' helps us to understand economic differences around the world.

Core processes include activities such as: car manufacture, scientific research, pharmaceuticals, aeronautical engineering, electronics, banking, insurance, stockbroking, government.

Peripheral processes include: mining and quarrying, cement production, paper production, market trading, assembly (only) of cars, assembly of computer equipment, heavy engineering.

All kinds of jobs occur in both core and peripheral processes, though the wages may be higher in core processes and core regions.

Clearly the location and proportions of the processes that are core or periphery are constantly changing. What is high-tech today is low-tech tomorrow. So thinking about the world in these terms will help us to see the possibility of change and not to assume the world is as it is because it must be so!

We do still have to make sure that our pupils understand the political reality of North/South world divisions. But core/periphery provides an *alternative* analysis that gets away from the stereotypes of the Third World.

Another advantage of the core/periphery concept is that it can be applied at any scale from local to global.

Global-scale core regions such as North America and Western Europe contain many smaller-scale core regions, for example the Berkshire 'Golden Valley' or Southern California. Other areas within the global cores are in fact peripheral. In the same way global-scale peripheral regions such as Latin America and Africa contain smaller-scale core regions such São Paulo or Dakar and Nairobi. The West Pacific Rim is a marvellous example of a region developing as a 'core' area.

Decision-making, at any scale, is far more likely to take place in a core area than on the periphery.

With the increasing distance, in terms of culture, experience and mileage, between decision-makers and those affected, the risk of divorcing decisions from non-economic effects increases too — and so it becomes more likely that justice will retreat even further.

At the same time there are forces working against the strengthening of core/periphery patterns. E-mail and the Internet are making peripheral areas attractive and practical locations for the decision-makers and some of their staff.

Development is resulting in an unequal world in which some areas enjoy rising standards of living while others stagnate and sink. The vast differences between rich and poor result partly from the distances between the decision-makers and those affected.

c) The interdependence of countries

The interdependence of countries reflects the functioning of the global economy. Trade has traditionally been the link between countries.

Ghana in the global economy

Many years ago the role of a country like Ghana was clearly defined. Its raw materials, e.g. gold, timber and cocoa, were exported to countries like Britain, usually with little or no processing taking place. Then in 1957, following independence, came the chance to break free from the poverty cycle caused by the link to the 'mother country'.

Today, Ghana's main exports are still gold, timber and cocoa, plus aluminium, and trade is mainly with Britain, Germany, USA and Nigeria. Not much has changed, and if anything the gap between rich and poor in Ghana has widened.

Hidden behind these broad facts is Ghana's desperate attempt to stimulate the growth of its own industries through both informal and formal links with other countries. These range from the well-publicised deal with the American-owned Kaiser Aluminium Company which led to the building of the Akosombo Dam, through smaller-scale, locally controlled enterprises such as the

You are a Ghanaian government minister and are faced with two possible ways firms can earn much needed foreign exchange to boost the economy.

Route 1

A businesswoman tells you two small villages outside Tamale have won a contract to supply Body Shop directly with shea nuts to make shea butter for skin-cream. The deal is worth £4 per kilo. Ghana has never exported shea nuts before.

Route 2

A well-known international timber company has offered £100 million to fell and process the oldest trees in an area of several square kilometres outside the forest reserves in the rainforest of the south-west. The company say they will bring their own experts and equipment and re-plant what they cut down.

1 How will the contract affect Ghanaians who wish to use or buy Ghanaian shea nuts or timber? Make a list of people affected and describe who would be worst hit.

2 How will the contract affect employment among Ghanaians in the two areas:
a) directly?
b) indirectly?

3 Is there a future in the link with Body Shop? Explain your answers.
Is there a future in the link with the timber company? Explain your answers.

4 What are the likely effects on the environment of the shea-nut deal?
What are the likely effects on the environment of the timber plan?

5 Who do you think is getting the best of each deal:
a) Ghana or Body Shop?
b) Ghana or the timber company?
Explain your answer.

6 Do you think either deal could harm Ghanaians in other associated industries, for instance furniture makers, rice importers?

7 **Either**
Now write a report to Parliament saying which contract you think the government should recommend and why. You could choose neither if you want. What might be the problem for a country like Ghana if you turned both down?

Or
In groups, choose the type of deal you think would be the best for Ghana. You might go for Body Shop or for the other kinds of development you know about — perhaps Lava importers or *Suame* magazine [case studies in *Kumasi and Beyond*, DEC (Birmingham) 1995]. Consider the effects on Ghana's economy, effects on the environment, and whether the deal is in Ghana's interests. Present your argument to the class.

opening of a Coca Cola plant at Kumasi, right down to the level of individuals making and trading goods through West Africa and beyond.

These developments must be seen against the backcloth of the actions of the International Monetary Fund and its effects in Ghana.

Ghana's international links illustrate the complexity of

> The IMF insists on 'economic adjustment' before it will lend. In Bolivia, Chile and Ghana, real wages have significantly declined during 'adjustment'.
>
> *World Development Report,* 1992

the global economy. For example, the shea-nut butter link recently established with Body Shop provides evidence of reciprocal trade and the promotion of non-traditional exports, which could include pineapples and tuna following a deal with Heinz. Thus, Ghana's economy could grow and diversify, while easing pressure on the local environment by possibly reducing traditional exports.

World-wide international links are at an all-time high, especially with the growth of multinational enterprises (MNEs). Of the largest 100 economic units in the world today, half are nation states, half are MNEs. These firms account for 75% of world commodity trade and up to 30%

> ROVER, THE LAST GREAT BRITISH CAR MAKER, SOLD TO A GERMAN GIANT
> Newspaper headline
> 'It doesn't matter who owns the company — we are all interested in the generation of wealth.'
> BMW Chairman, 1.2.94

of world GDP. Superficially, at least, the links can be beneficial to all concerned, as for instance in the construction of a Ford Escort, which involved 14 different countries in component manufacture. Some links, however, simply minimise costs and maximise profits for the MNE's home country.

The interdependence our pupils should instantly recognise is illustrated on the supermarket shelves. It is possible to buy the same products in retail outlets in almost every country, and when our pupils shop, they are likely to be purchasing items from around the world. Consumer colonialisation and cultural invasion is a characteristic of the twentieth century. The spread of McDonalds and the like across the globe appears relentless, as is the uniform wearing of trainers, 'shades' and a Sony Walkman.

'My God, you're right — it isn't a mirage'

DICKINSON, BRITAIN Reproduced from **Thin Black Lines,** DEC (Birmingham)

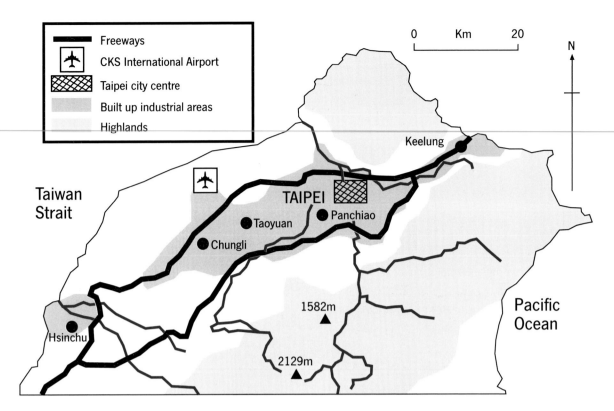

Location of Taipei, Taiwan

Globalisation

Walk round a big shopping centre in England and you can buy goods from dozens of different countries. You would find similar items in shops in New York or Nairobi, Rio or Delhi, Tokyo or Rome.

Look at your television, or take out a video, and all over the world you can see the same films, dubbed into different languages. News is beamed around the globe from space satellites. E-mail, faxes and the Internet provide instant communication world-wide. Politicians and businessmen jet-set from one five-star hotel to another, hardly knowing which country they are in. Holidaymakers routinely take global jaunts.

Behind all these activities which are stimulated and made possible by the expansion in global communications, are people and organisations with international global power. The transnational company (TNC), or the multinational enterprise (MNE), can control factories and the marketing of products in many countries. One bank can invest and lend money throughout the world; powerful countries' governments can influence what happens in other countries. An organisation can use television, print and advertising to persuade people in many countries to behave as they want them to.

All this is happening now. The process is called **globalisation**.

Mr Lin's comments (see panel) are in the context of this process, and the annotated map of Bawku shows how even a remote small town is linked into the global scene.

A TNC Chairman surveys the global scene

A message from Mr Lin, the Chairman of Tatung, the massive Taiwanese electrical manufacturer, based on an interview in Taipei in 1992 with Keith King and David Stanton of the Developing Geography group:

- Tatung shares the opportunities and concerns of Taiwan, and believes in its future prosperity.
- Tatung has an active policy of diversifying production and extending global links.
- Tatung has a loyal workforce, exemplifying the Confucian work ethic and its family values.
- Tatung will expand production in the Pacific Rim area as well as in Europe, the USA, and Sino-Russian regions.
- Tatung believes that the focus for the twenty-first century commercial market lies in the Pacific Rim where a new economic superstate will emerge.
- Tatung realises that this future is clouded by concerns for the environment.
- Tatung believes that its policy supporting education in the whole country can influence social problems and raise environmental awareness. Education is vital to economic success.
- Tatung realises that Taiwan is a high-income country with a dense population. This necessitates a high volume of economic activity to create commercial success, but in the long term it must move to a high-income/lower population density situation if growth is not to become strangled by congestion and pollution costs.

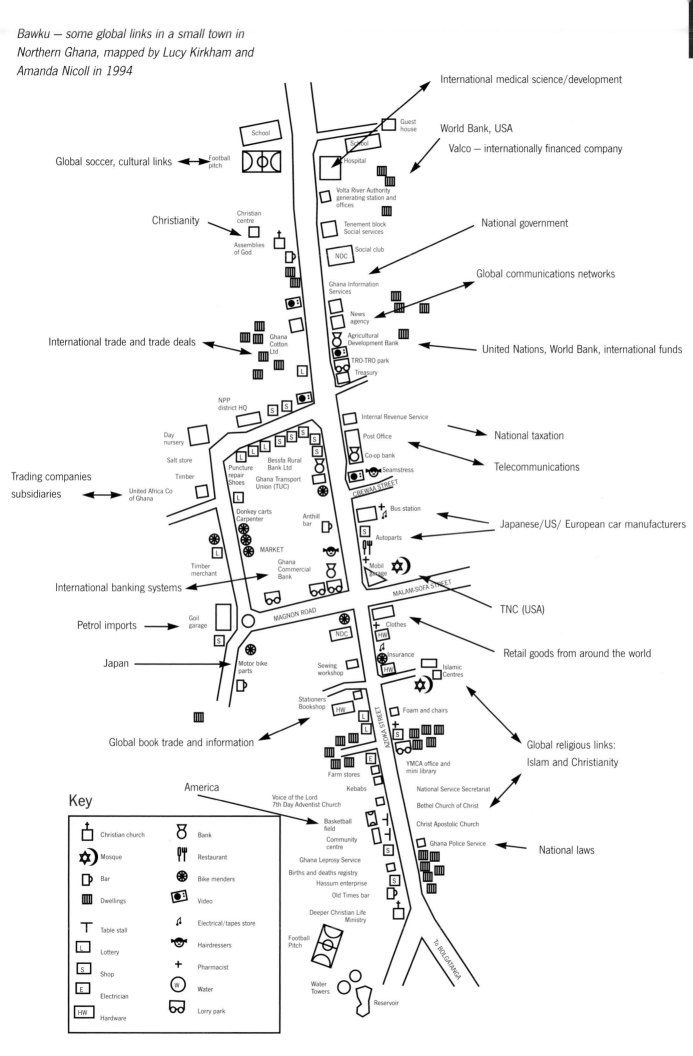

Bawku — some global links in a small town in Northern Ghana, mapped by Lucy Kirkham and Amanda Nicoll in 1994

International medical science/development

World Bank, USA

Valco — internationally financed company

Global soccer, cultural links

Christianity

National government

Global communications networks

International trade and trade deals

United Nations, World Bank, international funds

National taxation

Telecommunications

Trading companies subsidiaries

Japanese/US/ European car manufacturers

International banking systems

TNC (USA)

Petrol imports

Retail goods from around the world

Japan

Global religious links: Islam and Christianity

Global book trade and information

America

National laws

Key

Christian church	☩	Bank	⚕
Mosque	☪	Restaurant	🍴
Bar	▯	Bike menders	✹
Dwellings	▥	Video	▣
Table stall	T	Electrical/tapes store	♪
Lottery	L	Hairdressers	✂
Shop	S	Pharmacist	+
Electrician	E	Water	W
Hardware	HW	Lorry park	🚚

Guest house

School
School
Hospital
Volta River Authority generating station and offices
Tenement block Social services
NDC   Social club
Ghana Information Services
News agency
Agricultural Development Bank
TRO-TRO park
Treasury
Internal Revenue Service
Post Office
Co-op bank
Seamstress
NPP district HQ
Day nursery
Salt store
Timber
Bessfa Rural Bank Ltd
Ghana Transport Union (TUC)
Puncture repair Shoes
United Africa Co of Ghana
Ghana Cotton Ltd
Christian centre
Assemblies of God
Bus station
Autoparts
Mobil garage
Donkey carts Carpenter
Anthill bar
MARKET
Ghana Commercial Bank
Timber merchant
Goil garage
Clothes
HW
Insurance
HW
NDC
Islamic Centres
MAGNON ROAD
MALAM-SOFA STREET
CBEWAA STREET
AZOKA STREET
Motor bike parts
Sewing workshop
Stationers Bookshop
HW
Foam and chairs
Farm stores
YMCA office and mini library
Kebabs
National Service Secretariat
Voice of the Lord 7th Day Adventist Church
Bethel Church of Christ
Basketball field
Christ Apostolic Church
Community centre
Ghana Police Service
Ghana Leprosy Service
Births and deaths registry
Hassum enterprise
Old Times bar
Deeper Christian Life Ministry
Football Pitch
Water Towers
Reservoir
To BOLGATANGA

Wellcome Supermarket provides a case study of one TNC, while **How to invade a culture** offers pupils the opportunity to consider cultural invasion in more depth.

Wellcome Supermarket

The top management of Wellcome is white and Western-educated, from the UK, Australia and the USA. Below this are well-educated and well-qualified locals, and below this the local workforce. Wellcome imported the Western supermarket culture into one which was traditional but only too pleased to change.

In Wellcome supermarkets price is not the prime factor. Convenience, quality and variety are more important. 8000 items are available in each store. People shop about twice a week, because their homes are smaller than European homes and because they have less storage space and often no transport.

Each shop is almost indistinguishable from the Western version, except that the packaging has Chinese writing and the fish and fresh fruit and vegetable displays are much more exotic than you would find in Britain.

Hong Kong has 6 million people and 350 supermarkets. In Taiwan there are 20 million people and fewer than 200 supermarkets, so there is room for expansion. Finding new sites is tricky in the capital, Taipei, a busy, thriving city. City-centre space is short. At one time each new skyscraper had to have a bomb-shelter basement. These basements are now gradually being released for use as company premises because of the pressure of demand.

The buying manager

A typical member of the top management of Wellcome left Leeds Asda four months earlier and came to this growing area. He finds he has more responsibility, and is able to take decisions in situations where at home he would have to refer to higher authorities. As a young single man he is not concerned with schools, health or other social issues, and he does not see himself staying beyond his three-year contract. He sees the development of Taipei as outstripping the infrastructure, which is now struggling to catch up.

Wellcome Supermarket, Taipei, Taiwan

Stage 1 ...

Find a country with a growing economy and a traditional lifestyle.

Look carefully at the existing shopping pattern.

Find a site in a crowded city centre.

Fit it out in Western supermarket style.

Stock it with Western-style products, or, where products are local, package them in Western-style. The aim is for convenience, not lowest prices.

Be familiar with government rules — i.e. Ministry of Finance, Ministry of Economics — and banking practices.

Appoint a Finance Director, a Merchandising Director, a Buying Manager and a Human Resources Director, all with experience of Western retailing.

Stage 2 ...

Appoint a location hunter who knows the local area well and can seek new sites for further stores.

Appoint an Operations Director to handle customer service, train staff, take care of housekeeping, maintain the service level.

Commission a highly prestigious advertising campaign based on Western practice. Pay attention to local dialects. Use newspaper adverts, flyers and radio for advertising, as well as the exterior walls of the store.

Cash business only — do not accept cheques.

Find local suppliers for goods you wish to sell. Appoint staff to investigate possible new lines for the store, on the basis of one existing line out for each new one in.

Begin to insist on Western banking practices with your bank — e.g. paying suppliers by cheque, transferring funds electronically or by fax.

Set up a computer-based management information system. Install printer and terminal in each store for daily ordering.

Introduce an equal opportunities policy.

Look for expansion into other towns and cities.

Appoint a local understudy for each Western director.

How to invade a culture

Work with a colleague or group

1 Suppose you were involved in setting up a supermarket in Taiwan. What order of priority would you give to the items in stages 1 and 2? Put the cards from 'How to invade a culture' into the order you suggest. Compare your suggestions with those of other groups.

2 Do you think it is right for international companies to 'invade' other cultures like this?

3 Should communities safeguard their cultures from invasion? If so, how?

4 What are the dangers and advantages of having a global culture?

Activities

Main street in Taipei, Taiwan
Photo: Sandra Johnson

Predictions

Individuals and groups acting to bring about change can still have an effect on the future. Different priorities for development can be explored and their potential results discussed.

Spot the difference! provides pupils with the opportunity to consider alternative predictions about what could happen to an area in the future, and what factors are likely to influence its development.

- List as many differences as you can between the two pictures.
- What has happened to cause the situation in sketch one?
- Now focus on sketch two. What things need to happen within the local community or at government level to create the situation shown?

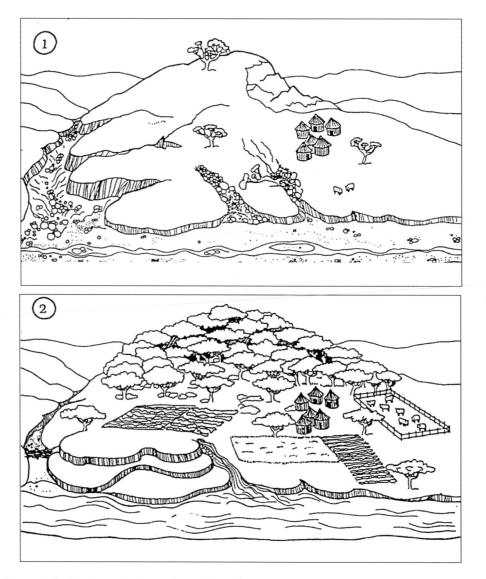

Spot the difference! An imaginary landscape in northern Ghana

So what is development?

The National Curriculum gives fairly precise pointers to what our pupils should be taught about development. Here we explore what those pointers indicate.

It is relatively easy to identify in Dearing's prescription, at least at a superficial level, what the pupils should be taught. However, we owe it to them, and to society, to go further than simply reinforcing the fact that differences in development exist. They need to consider aspects such as those listed in the panel.

What do we mean by development?

Why does development in Place A affect Place B? And how?

Who decides what development is and where it takes place?

Who gets what from development? And who loses what?

Is this development sustainable?

How does development happen?

Why does development in Place A look like this, but in Place B it's like that?

What is our role in development? Here?

Elsewhere in the world?

What effect does development have on us? - on other people? - on the environment?

What are the costs? (not just in terms of money)

If we engage pupils in considering such questions, we should recognise that economic growth does not automatically translate into a better quality of life, and that in recent years many have experienced growth without development. This directly challenges many of our basic assumptions about growth, development and the resulting quality of life. It also challenges what we mean by the word 'development'.

The eminent economist Dudley Seers has identified three vital aspects of development which serve to broaden the traditional view of development as economic growth, arguing that a decline in all three indicates that development is taking place. He asks us to consider:

1 What is happening to **poverty** in the country under study?
2 What is happening to **unemployment?**
3 What is happening to **inequality?**

The philosopher Denis Goulet challenges the notion of economic growth as development by positing three goals that should underpin development:

1 **Life sustenance** – food, health, shelter, protection
2 **Esteem** – the promotion of respect for all
3 **Freedom** – not only political, but in social, cultural, economic and spiritual matters.

Here development means liberation from economic, social and political factors which diminish people's quality of life. This view emphasises the ethical aspects involved, stressing the integrity, humanity and rights of individuals.

Birmingham Development Education Centre offers the following 'snowballing' definition of development:
- Development is about **people**.
- Development is about people making **choices**.
- Development is about people making choices based on **values**.
- Development is about people making choices based on values about the **quality of life**.

Chapter 3:
Planning
and Reviewing

The National Curriculum provides a context for planning key stage 3 work, but teachers still have a wide range of choices for the content, sequence and teaching/learning approaches of their courses and lessons.

It is all too easy to accept the readily available resources and textbooks and just teach from them as they come. Sometimes this works, but usually far more can be gained when teachers have been involved in the process of planning and have added their own creative stamp to the work.

Four planning tools are described here, and an in-service activity suggested for each.

The Trircle planner

The 'Trircle' is a circle divided into three sectors for use as a planning tool. It was 'invented' by a group of geography teachers on a DEC (Birmingham) study visit to the Gambia and Senegal in 1984, and has proved useful for clarifying aims and teaching methods for short units of work.

Using the Trircle makes us identify in detail what the main elements of a unit of work are to be, without losing sight of the complete package we are offering to the pupils.

The sectors of the Trircle could be called 'content', 'aims' and 'methods'. There are decisions to be made about the content of the work. The problem may be one of selecting possible content rather than identifying it. We are arguing for an approach which is learner-centred and gives importance to pupils' ideas, perceptions and values. We therefore need to consider our aims in this light. Finally, we also need to design teaching methods which are appropriate to these aims.

The illustration shows how the Trircle may be applied to a syllabus topic on population change.

By asking ourselves the question **'What do we hope our pupils will gain from the work on ...?'**, we are able to come up with ideas which are a closer reflection of practical classroom work. This gets us away from the broad aims which are a familiar introduction to many curriculum plans. It is therefore also easier to evaluate our aims and modify our plans accordingly. We can then review the learning activities in order to check that they are appropriate.

A group of teachers in Ghana used these planning tools to explore a syllabus topic

TRIRCLE PLANNER

Syllabus topic (or topics):

What focus? | What do we hope the student will gain? | What teaching activities?

TRIRCLE PLANNER

Syllabus topic/s: Components of population change

Relationship between population change and development

What focus? | What do we hope the student will gain? | What teaching activities?

To know and better appreciate:
A. the relationship existing between population change and development and their causative factors;
B. What this means in human terms.

- Brainstorming to make use of students' experiences

- Analysis of population data also using graphs

- Case studies and stories to illustrate figures

- Newspaper cuttings about current population debates

(The Trircle planner)

(Using the Trircle planner to explore 'Components of population change')

The Ghanaian teachers also used the Development Compass Rose to identify the major forces influencing their chosen focus: Population change and development.

Natural
Fertility, birth, death and infant mortality rates

Who decides?
Individual decision-making
ommunal decision-making
and Government decision-making

Economic
Growth rate of unemployment, pressure on land, cost of living and government spending

Social
Overcoming in urban areas, poor housing conditions, creation of shanty developments, higher crime rates, prostitution, traffic congestion and other pressure on social amenities and utilities

The Development Compass Rose and population change

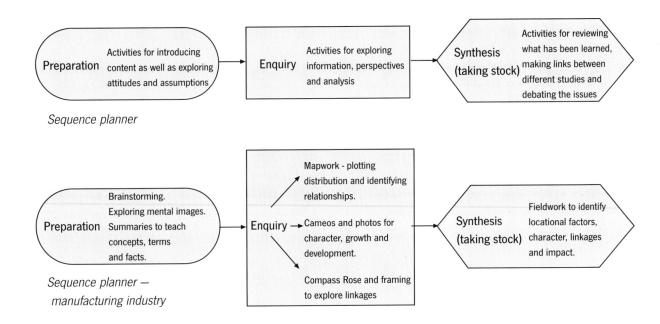

Sequence planner

Sequence planner –
manufacturing industry

Sequence planner

Planning a scheme of work in the sequence *Preparation > Enquiry > Synthesis* provides a natural context for developing enquiry-based lessons.

One group using this framework to outline a unit of work on manufacturing industry began by finding out what the pupils already knew of manufacturing, and at the same time introduced some basic terms and concepts.

Working in small groups, the pupils were asked first to provide their own definitions of a number of basic terms, e.g. *industry, manufacturing, scale, location* and *appropriate technology*. Then, having looked at photos or slides of a variety of manufacturing enterprises, they were asked to brainstorm why different factories are found in different locations. They tried to identify a series of location factors such as:

- **raw material** – timber, food products, minerals
- **labour** – skilled and unskilled
- **capital** – finance, machinery, appropriate technology
- **transport and communications** – roads, dock facilities
- **markets** – local, national, international
- **government policies** – tax holidays, credits
- **international and multinational linkages** – between suppliers, markets, financial.

A concluding class discussion attempted to identify what factors influence where manufacturing takes place. This completed the **Preparation** stage.

The **Enquiry** stage explored the extent to which the pupils' initial conclusions were found to be correct, by studying in detail a specific manufacturing industry.

The **Synthesis** included fieldwork based on a factory visit.

The matrix of themes and scales

Study and scales

The importance of study at different scales has been emphasised in the revised Order. The matrix of scales, part of which is shown, was used in SCAA conferences around the country. It can be used as a format for planning studies for key stage 3. There are two main pitfalls to be avoided:

1 Labels

First, the labels for the columns require interpretation. 'Local' in this context can be anywhere in the world — not necessarily local to the pupils and teacher — and 'Regional' here implies areas within nations rather than physical or climatic regions. 'National' is clear enough, and it is good that the revised Order accepts the political and economic realities of the nation-state as a basis for study.

The differences between 'International' and 'Global' are important but not clearly defined. Any activities or patterns involving two or more nations can be labelled 'international', so studies at this scale might be of the EU, or the British Isles, or of aid and trade between two countries. 'Global', on the other hand, implies processes that affect nations in patterns covering the whole world. Physical examples are obvious — climatic or geological processes, for example — but human examples are not so clear-cut. World economic processes and technological advances are examples, even though certain countries and areas may try to opt out of these systems.

This structure of scales, local to global, provides an excellent checklist for planning, even if in detail there can be some confusion.

	Local	Regional	National	International	Global
Thematic Studies For example:					
Settlement					
Economic activities					
Development	←	←	←	←	X
Place Studies					
Country A	←	X	X	X	→

X   specified focus in the new Order

←   necessary connections

Filling in the blanks
Extract from key stage 3 matrix of scales (from *National Curriculum Consultation Geography,* SCAA)

2 Scale linkages

The second pitfall concerns the way the matrix might be used as a planning tool. It has sometimes been used to select a spread of both 'issues' and 'places' for study, and some muddled thought has resulted. Most problems come from the implication that it is possible to choose to study a specific place at a particular scale, ignoring the other scales for that study. This is completely at variance with the whole point of emphasising different scales and the relationships between processes at different scales. Take an example at 'local' scale — the study of economic activity in an inner-city area (contributing to the delivery of key stage 3 themes of Settlement, Economic activities and Development).

Sparkbrook, Birmingham, could be used as a case study. Sparkbrook has a male unemployment level of nearly 50%; it has been at this level for more than five years. (33,000 people in central Birmingham have been out of work for more than one year.) Local-scale study could emphasise enterprise schemes, redevelopments, work in the informal economy, and local initiatives. But any real understanding of the state of the inner city must relate it to international and global economic processes which have made high unemployment endemic in Britain,

and to the national economic and social systems that have concentrated this in the inner cities. Without reference to these larger-scale processes (including multinational company policies, trade agreements and international finance), not only is understanding impossible, but the hidden messages about the people in the inner cities are very negative.

While no local- or regional-scale place study can be meaningful without reference to national and global processes, place studies at any scale above 'local' need reference to specific local examples of people and places to which pupils can relate as part of the real world. For example, pupils studying 'contrasting regions' of, say, Ghana, cannot grasp the reality of those regions if they have not had the chance to find out about specific places and learn about the lives of the people there.

To sum up: when using the matrix, by all means focus on study at a chosen scale, but in each study always:
- go **up** the whole scale for understanding of process
- and come all the way **down** to local scale to learn about the reality of place and people.

Experience suggests that most teachers find this matrix useful as a checking device after drafting a plan for teaching, revising the plan in the light of it. It can also be

	Home area and region	UK and European Union	The wider world
Local		Development of holiday homes in the Peak District.	Rural depopulation as migrant workers move to Johannesburg (South Africa).
Regional		Effect of opening the M40 and increased possibility of commuting to London from Warwickshire.	Migrant workers in South Africa. Quality of life in Johannesburg.
National, International and Global		Migrant workers in Europe.	World population movements — Ethiopian Jews to Israel, Boat People in south-east Asia.

Case study: area focus
The matrix suggests an approach for the theme of Migration.

used as an overall check for balance in longer schemes of work and for the key stage 3 programme as a whole.

Planning a small unit of work on a particular theme can be helped by using the matrix, because it emphasises the links between scales and at the same time draws attention to the importance of studies focused at different scales.

Reviewing

The scale matrix can have the dual function of planning and reviewing, but there are key questions that can be asked about content and methods to evaluate the development perspective.

Content review

In what ways is the environment being used/changed and what resources are being exploited/developed?

1 What relationships between the community and the environment are or were maintained by traditions and indigenous technology?
2 Is the environment being degraded/polluted/ exploited/conserved/improved? If so, by whom? For whose benefit?
3 Which processes within the ecosystem will be changed/disrupted/improved by the development?
4 Who benefits and by how much during the resource development? Who suffers or fails to benefit?
5 How do outside links affect activities? To whose advantage do they operate?
6 Is the resource development sustainable? If not, what will happen when the resource is exhausted?
7 Are exploitation and conservation mutually exclusive?

What change has taken/is taking place?

1 How far is change the result of outside influence, how far due to local initiative?
2 How are new technologies changing the relationship between the community and the environment?
3 How have particular people/groups been affected by change?
4 Are traditional patterns represented as inferior? Is 'West best'? By what criteria?
5 Does change lead to economic or social well-being for a large proportion of the people living in the local area?

What obvious patterns of social/spatial inequality exist?

1 How do you measure inequality?
2 Are there groups which are especially advantaged or disadvantaged?
3 Are there groups which are identified as inferior/superior? By what criteria?
4 How even is the distribution of opportunity, education, services, wealth and resources in the study area?
5 Do outside agencies actively promote changes in economic/social/cultural patterns? Who decides?
6 What processes lead to these social/spatial inequalities?

Who owns and controls the land, buildings and enterprises? Who holds the power?

1 How far are local people involved in decisions affecting the area?
2 Who is managing/providing capital for the resource development?
3 How is the supply of money, labour and land for enterprises organised and controlled?
4 How do those in power maintain control? Can individuals expect justice?
5 Who controls trade, marketing and distribution of goods?
6 Are alternative power, control and ownership systems acknowledged or considered?

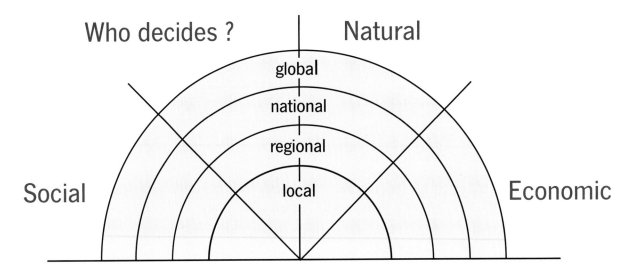

The Compass Rose and scales

The Development Compass Rose and content review

The Development Compass Rose can be used to review the approach to specific case studies or examples to ensure that all the dimensions of development are considered. Each piece of work is likely to emphasise only some of the dimensions, but it is important not to forget the others and to dig deep enough in each direction.

The Compass Rose can be combined with the scale matrix to check out coverage of dimensions at different scales.

Methods review

Teaching methods should also be reviewed, and of course 'variety is the spice of life'. Over a period of weeks some balance might be expected between different approaches.

Key questions on 'methods'

Here are some key questions to review methods of teaching and resources.

Do the teaching methods and resources ...

1   provide opportunity for work and discussion between pupils:
    a) for individual enquiry
    b) for group presentation
    c) for individual presentation?
2   provide a variety of descriptive material:
    a) video
    b) photographs, pictures, cartoons
    c) graphs
    d) tables
    e) written accounts?
3   give perspectives that include:
    a) individual/family initiatives
    b) alternative value and attitudes
    c) alternative economic and social situations?

Do the pupil activities ...

- give the pupils ownership of their study?
- encourage wide ranging and open questioning?
- encourage careful and logical analysis?
- lead to some kind of synthesis and evaluation?

Teacher planning activities

Teacher activity: Using a Trircle

1 Copy the diagram on page 39.
2 Choose a key stage 3 curriculum topic from the syllabus.
3 Write down your initial assumption about the focus.
4 Complete the sentence: 'We hope the pupils will gain ... ' (It is important to use everyday language.)
5 Consider what you have written already, and think about what teaching activities would enable you to do this.
6 Having completed your ideas, it is important to go back and reconsider each box and develop the initial ideas. Perhaps use the Compass Rose to explore the focus more deeply. See if you can sharpen up the plan.

Teacher activity: Outlining an enquiry-based unit of work

1 Choose a key stage 3 topic to which a series of several lessons will be devoted.
2 Outline a sequence of work based on *preparation > enquiry > synthesis*.
3 Decide in more detail how the results of the enquiry will be shared for synthesis.

Teacher activity: Themes and scales

1 Choose a topic to be studied for the theme of development.
2 Select a scale as focus and select a case study at this scale.
3 Discuss the links to other scales and other themes.
4 Review the choice of this scale as focus and of this case study in the light of the links discussed.

Teacher activity: Using key questions

1 Use the key questions on both content and method to review a unit of work which you have recently taught.
2 Revise the unit in the light of the review and if necessary to take more account of a development-education perspective.

Chapter 4:
Foundations
of Enquiry

The National Curriculum

wholeheartedly supports enquiry

learning. This chapter suggests

specific activities and techniques

that can lead to successful enquiry

learning in geography. It includes

methods that can be used to

enquire into all manner of content

with a wide variety of resources.

The methods are equally useful

with pupils outside the key stage 3

age range.

Discussion and working together

Discussion between pupil and pupil, as well as between pupil and teacher, is at the heart of enquiry learning.

Pupils should be given the opportunity to learn how to:

- express and justify feelings, opinions and viewpoints with increasing sophistication
- discuss increasingly complex issues
- assess and interpret arguments and opinions with increasing precision and discrimination
- present their ideas, experiences and understanding in a widening range of contexts across the curriculum and with an increasing awareness of audience and purpose
- ask increasingly precise or detailed questions
- present factual information in a clear and logically structured manner in a widening range of situations – discriminate between fact and opinion and between relevance and irrelevance, and recognise bias
- use, and understand the use of, role-play in teaching and learning
- communicate with other group members in a wide range of situations
- discuss issues in small and large groups, taking account of the views of others, and negotiating a consensus
- report and summarise in a range of contexts
- reflect on their own effectiveness in the use of the spoken word
- engage in prediction, speculation and hypothesis in the course of group activity.

The range of opportunities provided should:

- allow pupils to work in groups of various sizes, both single-gender and mixed where possible, with and without direct teacher supervision.

	Through discussion pupils can learn to use their experience or knowledge as a basis from which to express an opinion.	
Discussion helps pupils express their views orally.	Through discussion pupils can learn to use their experience or knowledge as a basis from which to express an opinion.	Through discussion pupils can learn to speak confidently to an audience.
Discussion gives pupils opportunities to become aware of their own needs and to clarify them.	Through discussion pupils can respond freely in their own terms.	Discussion allows pupils to express their considered views and justify them openly to their peers and the teacher.
Discussion can encourage pupils to listen carefully to the views of peers.	Through discussion pupils can learn to concentrate on the subject under consideration.	Discussion enables pupils to respond to the views of others — to support or reject them, or to modify their own ideas.

Teacher activity: Discussing 'discussion'

One way of doing this is a ranking exercise, when the sharing of ideas is based around the group task of arranging statements into the shape of a diamond. Two sets of statements relating to discussion in the classroom are provided, based on answers to the questions **What does discussion bring to the classroom?** and **Why is group work important for pupils?**

Take each of these statement sets separately.

1 Working in groups of three or four, arrange the **What does discussion bring to the classroom?** statements according to which the group agrees with. The one securing the most agreement is placed at the top of the diamond, the next two are ranked equal second, and so on until the one with least support is placed at the bottom.

   This will encourage the pupils to discuss each statement, justify their viewpoints and listen to each other's ideas.

What does discussion bring to the classroom?

   A plenary discussion should be used to bring the groups together.

2 Working with the **Why is group work important for pupils?** series of statements:

   Discuss the suggestions about the importance of group work.

   Add your own suggestions.

   Which of the statements would also apply to discussion in pairs?

3 Choose a development issue as a topic and decide what kind of resources are necessary to promote the learning suggested for group work.

For effective learning

Group work promotes more efficient learning than competition or individual work. It encourages the creative sharing and generating of ideas.

For working together

Learning can be too individualised, so it is important to develop opportunities for working together. Through group work pupils can develop skills of self confidence, communication and co-operation. Small groups maximise opportunities for building skills.

For open-ended learning

Although a task or stimulus may be the focus of group work these methods offer opportunities for pupils to explore areas they are interested in at their own levels. They allow pupils to take more responsibility for their own learning and to control it better.

For confidence-building

It takes confidence to share opinions or ideas in a class discussion — group work can help pupils to test out their thoughts on others and clarify their ideas. Talk is a very valuable medium for sorting out your own ideas.

For building enthusiasm

Children enjoy participating ... in assemblies hands shoot up when volunteers are needed. Group work, which involves being active for a large proportion of the time, is an opportunity to respond to their enthusiasm and motivation.

For learning to value their own experience

All pupils come to school with a wealth of experience. They need to learn that they have important things to say and share with others.

For promoting equal opportunities

Children with special needs may be catered for by creating different sorts of groups and partnerships. A bilingual child whose first language is Urdu, for example, may have more opportunity to contribute in an Urdu-speaking group. Girls may benefit from sometimes working in single-gender groups.

Why is group work important for pupils?

Exploring assumptions and images

In order to stimulate pupils to explore some of their basic assumptions and attitudes about a place or situation, you need some activities which clearly indicate that you are not seeking particular answers. You also need to encourage them to recognise that they do have assumptions about particular places, and to be aware that others in the class might have different assumptions.

Some activities follow:

Expectations

'Expectations' is an activity giving pupils an opportunity to express their ideas about an area of the world or a topic which is about to be studied. The views that are expressed will give an indication of the attitudes that pupils may have towards the subject and also any knowledge they have about it.

Expectations enables the teacher:

- to find out what the pupils already know about the subject
- to gain some indication of the pupils' attitudes
- to introduce discussion techniques
- to establish the idea that pupils can learn from each other.

It is useful to introduce the topic by using leading questions. These provide a trigger for the pupils' thoughts. It is important that these questions should enable an open-ended response.

'The questioning game'

For 'The questioning game' pupils are told that they have been landed by parachute in, say, India. They are asked to discuss with a partner the things that they would want to find out, and each writes a list of questions they would like answered. These are useful for finding out the things that are of concern to the pupils and for reference at a future date to see whether pupils' ideas, images and attitudes have altered as a result of the course.

What do you expect?

We are going to look at _____

in our geography lessons in the next few weeks.

1 Has _____

been in the newspaper recently? What for?

2 Have any particular places been mentioned? Why? What happened?

3 What is _____

famous for? or known for?

Now get into pairs. You have a few minutes to get as many ideas or questions about _____ as you can think of! Imagine you have just landed in _____ by parachute, what would you most like to know about the area and the people?

List of questions

- _____
- _____
- _____
- _____
- _____

A pupil prompt sheet for 'Expectations' and 'The questioning game'

This part of the activity enables pupils to:

- share ideas with their peers
- discuss attitudes and opinions informally
- explore images in more detail.

Comments

The final part of the session gives pupils a chance to share their ideas, attitudes and images of India with the rest of the class. Selected lists are read out and pupils are allowed to comment on how their questions agreed or disagreed with those that have been read aloud. Pupils are encouraged to make observations on the comments of their classmates.

The final section of the activity:

- helps participants to discover areas of agreement/disagreement
- encourages pupils to listen to each other
- gives opportunities for pupils to respond to each other's ideas
- clarifies the participants' learning needs.

While most pupils have images of places they know little about, they probably realise that they base these on a small amount of experience or evidence. When it comes to a place they feel they know, things may be different and their assumptions about what it is like can be much firmer.

A collection of emotive adjectives (both positive and negative) such as those shown with the map of Britain can be used to stimulate discussion about assumptions.

1 Ask pupils to suggest words and write a complete list on the blackboard.

2 Ask pupils to select ten words, five of which they think are positive and five negative.

3 Write each word on a small scrap of paper and place it on the map. (A map of Britain could be used, or alternatively a more local one or a world map.)

4 Each group could then be asked to share their map with the rest of the class, highlighting:
   a) which words they have used
   b) where they have placed them
   c) which labels were difficult to place
   d) which places were difficult to label.

5 This feedback could generate much discussion. It would be useful to focus on the extent to which the views expressed are justified, and, if so, from whose point of view. It is also important to encourage discussion about what might influence our images of

Photo-images and attitudes

This activity is a technique for becoming aware of how attitudes and expectations affect what we see. It shows how interpretation of visual images can be biased by what we expect to find in them.

A slide or photograph can be used. A photograph in a set of textbooks is often more manageable than a single photograph which may not be easily seen by the whole class, or a single slide which requires a projector to be set up.

Ideal images are those which show a contrast between modern and traditional aspects of life, or challenge stereotypes. A selection of published photopacks is listed in the Appendix.

The activity enables the teacher:
• to learn more about pupils' reactions to modern and traditional aspects of life
• to assess their attitudes towards wealth and poverty
• to recognise the stereotyping and prejudices to which the pupils have been exposed.

Procedure for pupil activity

1 Up to six members of the class are asked to leave the room.
2 The image is shown to the remainder of the class.
3 After they have had time to assimilate its content, the image is removed.
4 One of the pupils is asked to return, and the class describe what they have seen.
5 The second outsider returns and the first describes what s/he has just been told.
6 This process continues, bringing one person in at a time, until the 'image' has been described to all those who had been asked to leave.

While the descriptions are being given, the observers (the remainder of the class) note which features have been transmitted accurately, which have been changed, and the details that have been omitted.

The whole class is then asked to look carefully at the image. Pupils will probably be amazed by what is actually shown on it. Both what they have remembered, and what has been described, may have little relationship to the original photograph.

The activity concludes with discussion about the changes, misinterpretations and differing points that have emerged regarding the original image.

The process could also be applied to the way in which some newspaper articles are written.

This activity enables pupils:
• to respond in their own terms
• to become aware of their own attitudes to the place/issue/people being considered
• to recognise the different viewpoints expressed by their peers.

Myth-busting

Some development themes have entered the public consciousness through the media and have assumed mythical status. Challenging popular myths encourages the pupils to think critically about supposed causes and effects.

'Learning begins with unlearning: myths must be unlearned before complexity can be understood.'

It is possible that a pupil may express an attitude which the teacher cannot condone; there are likely to be more pupils who hold beliefs of a similar nature.

Prejudiced views may be countered if the teacher is able to introduce evidence that encourages the pupils to reconsider — the teacher may well have to become a myth-buster.

Inappropriate labelling, and incomplete or false images, perpetuate popular myths.

Teacher activity: Develop a true/false game

Use **Myths of world hunger**, quoted in Chapter 2 pages 26–27, to create a true/false game about population and food for key stage 3 pupils.

Sorting and matching activities

Sorting activities involve making decisions about how to group a variety of statements, objects, pictures, etc.

They are useful techniques for:

- encouraging pupils to co-operate in making choices
- discussing a range of points of view — and therefore very valuable for issue-centred learning
- showing the pupils that items can be sorted into many different sub-sets
- developing discussion skills such as criticising, judging, defending, arguing, listening, comparing and contrasting.

Sorting is a familiar activity to those who work with young pupils. It holds great potential for issue-centred work. There are many variations on the same theme. The basis of the activity lies in organising the items into two or more groups. These groups can be suggested by the teacher or the pupils can define their own.

Sorting objects

Give the pupils a set of objects. They could include objects from different parts of the world, from the past and present, or objects which at first seem to have no obvious connection with each other. These are some examples of the objects you could use:

- fresh food, such as fruits and vegetables, including those grown in other parts of the world
- household items from different parts of the world
- toys
- a shopping basket of food
- a bag of clothes with labels of countries of manufacture.

An initial activity might be to ask the pupils to sort the objects into two groups. When they have done this, you could ask them to try to sort them into two different groups. This may be much more difficult, as they will have to dismantle the first sets and think up different groupings.

Another way of using the objects would be first to ask the pupils to sort them into three sets. This is usually more challenging than sorting into two, as they cannot use opposites such as old/new or large/small as criteria. It is likely to create much more imaginative discussion.

Sorting statements

When developing a theme around an issue, it is important that the pupils are aware that people hold different points of view. Give the pupils a set of statements showing various viewpoints, and ask them to sort them into those they agree with and those they disagree with.

When they have sorted and discussed the statements, the pupils could add their own. Alternatively, in pairs, one could argue in favour and the other against a particular statement.

Using Venn diagrams

These are a valuable structure for sorting ideas and items. The one below can be used when you are looking at the future dimensions of an issue. If you are looking at the contributors to acid rain, river pollution and ocean pollution, you could give the pupils a list of what factors might contribute and ask them to place them on the diagram.

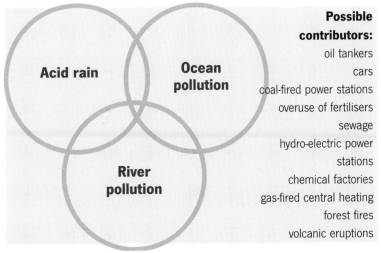

Possible contributors:

oil tankers
cars
coal-fired power stations
overuse of fertilisers
sewage
hydro-electric power stations
chemical factories
gas-fired central heating
forest fires
volcanic eruptions

Using a Venn diagram

Teacher activity: Try a matching exercise

1 Read the report 'Multinational on the move' in the panel. The resources here have been taken from *The Global Money Machine,* DEC (Birmingham), 1994.

2 Put the *People's profiles* and *initial reactions* on two sets of cards.

3 Who said what? Match the people with their initial reactions. What does this say about the issue of multinationals and the relocation of factories?

4 Evaluate this exercise — the issue and the people are real, but the opinions are made up using the author's personal knowledge of the people. What do you think about this? In school textbooks there are many made-up sections, usually based on reality. Does this matter? Is it vital to explain this to the pupils?

Twenty years ago an American electronics company moved to Taiwan. The labour costs were low, and with help from the Taiwanese government they could have a brand-new factory with the latest machinery making low-cost, reliable electronic components. Many workers were very loyal, and the factory expanded — a real success story for electronics and Taiwan.

However, 20 years later the workers noticed that the machinery was gradually disappearing from the factory. 'Where is it going?' they asked. 'It was rented and had to be returned' they were told.

The truth was different. The machinery was being exported by ship to Mexico to equip a new factory. During a holiday in Taiwan the rest of the machines disappeared. A horror story was in the making for electronics and Taiwan!

'Why move our factory to Mexico?' asked the workers. 'What about us?'

Imagine their feelings when they were told the reasons for moving. The company needed a brand-new factory, where labour costs were low, to be able to produce low-cost, reliable electronic components. It would be a real success story for electronics and Mexico.

'But what about the 20 years of service we have given the company?' asked the workers. 'Aren't you still making a lot of money from the electronics in Taiwan?'

'But we can make more money in Mexico,' replied the factory owners, 'labour costs are lower!'

Multinational on the move: America, Mexico and Taiwan

Ulysses Cheng
The human resources manager of a large electronics firm in Taipei. He is 40 years old and married with two children aged 5 and 3. His wife is a teacher at the local junior school. He often works a 14-hour day and a six-day week. On Sunday he relaxes with his family in the local mountains. He has done two years' military service in the air force.

Mary Li
Aged 24, Mary is a pupil at Taipei University studying for a Master's degree. She speaks Taiwanese, Mandarin and English fluently. She wants to be a social worker. Her parents have arranged a marriage for her. She does not follow any religion. Her father is a successful businessman. Her mother also works as a businesswoman in the same company. Mary's main sport is baseball.

Shaun Casey
Irish Roman Catholic priest who speaks and writes fluent Taiwanese. He lives in Taoyuan, an industrial area in northern Taiwan. He cares for immigrants, exploited workers and children sold into prostitution. He is deeply concerned for these people.

Mrs Chou
38 years old, of aboriginal Taiwanese/Chinese descent, Mrs Chou is married to a Christian pastor. Her family live in a fruit-growing area in the mountains. She lives in Taipei and has three teenage children. She works with aboriginal people who have recently migrated to the city.

Mr Chung
Born in 1935, Mr Chung had a hard childhood during the Japanese occupation. In 1954 he saw military action in the Penghu islands against the Chinese mainlanders; he was shelled continually for two months. This left him shellshocked. In 1955 he married a local farmgirl who taught him the basics of farming. They have worked extremely hard on their farm for the last 40 years. This has allowed them to buy a large seven-bedroomed house and to enjoy a good lifestyle. They now have four sons who have a variety of careers.

'This is a difficult problem: if companies don't continually cut costs they are liable to go out of business in this competitive world.'

'The alternative to closing down is to invite more foreign workers from countries like Sri Lanka and Vietnam to work here for very low wages and often in bad conditions. I'm not sure this is any better.'

'Young people must work hard and gain qualifications that will make sure they can get jobs that cannot be done by unskilled cheap labour abroad.'

'This is hard on the workers who have to fight for a job and recognition. Many haven't had the chance of education, and even with a job their low pay means they live in poor conditions.'

'I feel sorry for these workers. It is quite likely that they were forced to move to the city from farming when mechanisation came in, and now with more change they are bearing the brunt of suffering again.'

Left: People profiles
Above: Initial reactions

Using key questions

The essence of enquiry learning is asking questions. Learning to ask the relevant, or as some would say the 'right', question is the most important skill to develop with pupils. However, they need experience using 'key' questions which have been developed and applied to a variety of geographical situations . This helps them to explore issues and to develop their own questioning skills.

An example of key questions about **Justice and economic activity** is given here. The questions are not meant to be used simply as classroom worksheets, though this may sometimes be appropriate. They are meant as a resource which teachers can use separately or collectively in a variety of ways.

The key questions are useful checklists for teachers preparing lessons and selecting resources, and as follow-up or revision for pupils at the end of a piece of work.

They can also be used as an integral part of enquiry-based learning. The pupils can be encouraged to ask these questions explicitly during some lessons, to discuss them with their peers, and to keep them at the back of their minds on other occasions.

The questions marked 'deeper study' often need special background knowledge, so they may need to be modified for application to specific case studies and simplified for use with some pupils.

Major questions could become part of everyday thinking. They can be applied informally and quickly to make sure that they are not being forgotten in an approach to a subject or topic, or used as a checklist to help with evaluation of a textbook or lesson resources.

KEY QUESTIONS

IS IT FAIR?

1 Is everyone having a fair share?
2 If not, what is preventing fair shares
   a) people?   b) circumstances?
   c) background and history?   d) lack of opportunity?
3 Why is this not fair? Should it be fairer? What ought to be done?
4 Are the economic activities fair to the people involved in them?

Is it fair? Deeper study 1

1 Is everyone having a fair share?

2 What do you think would be a fair share for each person/group of people/community/nation mentioned?

3 Why is this your idea of a fair share?
   a) List the things you have taken into account.
   b) Why do you think this?

Is it fair? Deeper study 4

1 Are the activities fair to the people involved in them?
   a) Do the people have fair conditions of work?
   b) Do the people involved get a fair reward for their efforts?
   c) Can the people involved influence decisions about the activity?

Is it fair? Deeper study 2

(If everyone is not having a fair share)
1 What is preventing fair shares?
2 Are people preventing fair shares?
   a) How do they do this?
   b) Why do they do this?
3 Are background and history preventing fair shares?
   a) Whose background and history is causing this?
   b) How does this prevent fair shares?
4 Are circumstances or lack of opportunity preventing fair shares?
   a) What is unfair about them?
(If everyone is having a fair share)
1 What is creating fair shares?
   a) Has this been organised on purpose?
   b) How has it been organised?
   c) Does anyone want it changed? Why?

Is it fair? Deeper study 3

(If everyone is not having a fair share)
1 Why is this not fair? Should it be fairer? What ought to be done?

2 Will making it fairer make things less good for some people? Is this a good idea?

3 Make a list of possible changes.
   a) How could each change be made?
   b) Who would have to agree?

4 Which changes do you personally think should happen?
   a) Whose interest did you put first?
   b) Agree a rank order for the possible changes.

Justice and economic activity

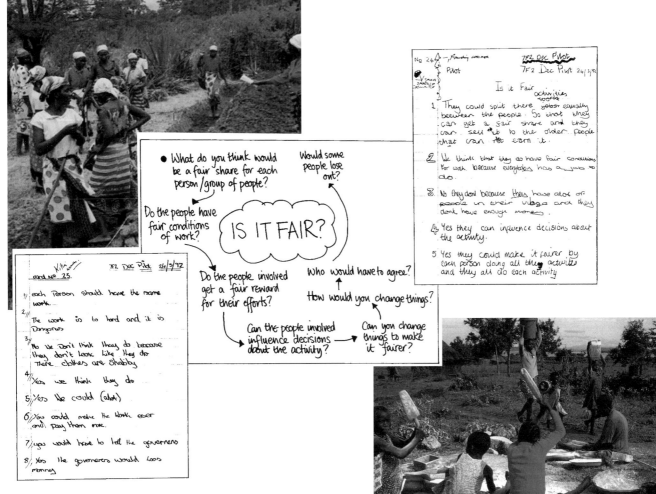

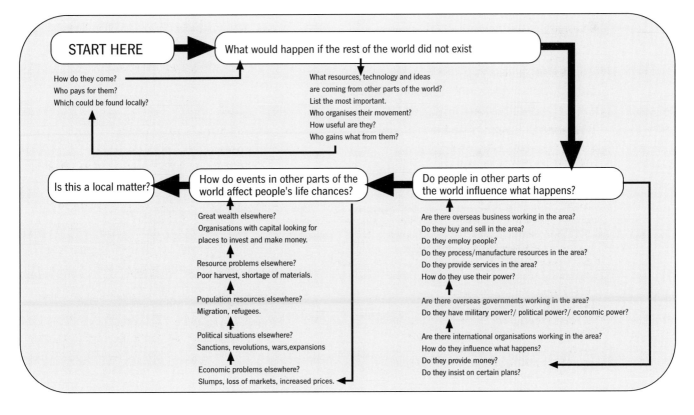

Global links — question trail

Teacher activity: Writing key questions

The management of H. J. Heinz and Company International has declared its intention to undertake a major business in Ghana that will make it the principal supplier of tuna and other fish products to Europe.

Dr H. J. O'Reilly, president and chief executive of Heinz, also promised to explore the industry in the country for the sake of the environment.

Dr O'Reilly named the other areas to be explored as pineapple and tomato processing.

The company is a global food processor with sales over seven billion dollars which operates in more than 200 countries .

'We think this is the best place to be in West Africa,' he added. Ghana's President Rawlings said a lot of crops harvested go to waste due to lack of processing as well as preservation facilities and this constitutes a deficit food supply because government alone could not purchase all that farmers produced.

President Rawlings said Ghana would welcome any investment in this area.

Ghana is trying to build up confidence but company names like Heinz on the processing front would be of advantage to the country in the export drive.

Daily Graphic (Accra) Monday 11 July 1994

Heinz to invest in Ghana

1 Consider the newspaper article *Heinz to invest in Ghana*.

2 Write a series of key questions to help pupils consider the issues involved in this development initiative.

Development Compass Rose

Using the Development Compass Rose (see pages 12 and 38–39) will help when you have a case study or issue that you want to explore in detail. The stimulus could be written material, a map, a photograph, or any combination of the three. It may be useful for pupils to draw their own copy of the Compass Rose (including the notes).

A typical sequence using the Development Compass Rose

• Explain the idea of the Development Compass Rose. The compass points (N, S, E and W) make it easier for pupils to remember.
• Introduce the case study.
• Split the class into small discussion groups.
• Ask each group to suggest questions (and write them down) to explore the case study from the different points of the compass. Encourage them to think about questions on the diagonal points (e.g. NE), which focus on the interrelationship between different factors.
• Ask groups to share some of their questions. Build up a class Compass Rose on the blackboard.
• Discuss how to find out about a selection of the questions.

Teacher activity

1 Choose an interesting photograph and fix it to the centre of a large piece of paper. Label the directions N, E, S and W. Brainstorm as many questions as possible about the photo and the situation portrayed.

2 Take another piece of paper and put the photo at bottom centre. Draw a diagram similar to the illustration on page 44. For each direction identify links and relationships at different scales that relate to your questions. Write them down, with 'local' nearest to the photo.

Photo activities – looking and seeing

As teachers, we may not like the idea that many of our pupils will acquire most of their knowledge and perceptions of the wider world from visual images. However, it is a fact and we cannot ignore it.

Visual presentations of information have an immediate appeal and invoke a quicker reaction than the written word. It is important, therefore, that we should make full and effective use of such material. Pupils' reactions should be explored and opportunities given for them to share ideas. Use of visual material should not be random, but carefully determined in advance.

The use of photographic material in teaching involves the development of learning skills. These include:

- making careful visual observations and verbal comments
- acquiring information from a visual source
- analysing and evaluating information
- relating one's own views to the image
- recognising the value of different interpretations
- producing a written or oral interpretation of an image
- empathising with the people or situations portrayed
- forming links between photographs.

Such skills should be built up gradually. Before pupils can learn from photographs, they must be given opportunities to look carefully. Both general impressions and detailed analyses are necessary. Until pupils have learned to assimilate the content of a picture, they will not be able to relate their own experiences.

Using visual materials gives pupils the opportunity:

- to respond freely regarding likes/dislikes, opinions, interests, evaluation
- to clarify their own attitudes towards the image
- to examine the lesson material in terms of its assumptions, bias and validity.

Playing in floods, Indonesia
Photo: Jeremy Hartley, Oxfam; source: *Focus on Stories*, Severn Trent, 1995.

Work with visuals usually involves the use of a published photopack or series of slides, although personal collections are also valuable.

Display boards are an excellent way of presenting photographs, particularly if the whole set needs to be visible.

Depending on the activities, other materials may also be necessary, e.g. lists of key words for labelling exercises, question grids for detailed photo-analysis.

Photograph exercises often involve different groupings within a single lesson. This has implications for the arrangement of furniture.

It is important to recognise that pupils often find it difficult to accept that there is no clear answer to a question. Teachers will need to help pupils to explore the diversity of opinions, rather than allowing them to come to a quick consensus.

Here we outline eight activities. The first introduces the idea of the photographic image. The remaining seven activities could be used with almost any photograph.

It is important to give time to some basic activities before considering bigger issues. By doing this pupils will be able to discover things for themselves from the photographs, rather than using them to illustrate points that you, as a teacher, are making.

Activities 2–4 emphasise 'looking and seeing'. Activities 5–8 involve analysis, interpretation and prediction.

Some activities can be adapted for use during or at the end of a piece of work, when the understanding and knowledge that pupils have gained can be used for review and synthesis. Activity 8 exemplifies this approach.

Activity 1: Framing an image

The school grounds, or the area very close by, offers a very accessible source for exploring development issues and the pupils' own views about them.

Using a frame helps pupils to focus their thinking and to go deeper than basic observation. The key questions support the pupils in thinking about the view in different ways.

1   Ask the pupils to get into groups of two or three.
2   The first stage is making the frame:
    a)   each pair has a sheet of paper in which they carefully cut out an oblong about 90 mm x 60 mm in the middle
    b)   discuss what questions they might wish to ask
    c)   write these key questions around the hole in the paper.
3   Suggest that the group go to different parts of the school grounds. Encourage them to experiment in choosing different views (even of things that seem quite boring in the first place).
4   Ask them to choose one view and to write notes in response to the key questions, and to draw a quick sketch of the main features in the frame.
5   Back in the class, they could prepare a short presentation describing their frame and some of the main issues arising.

This will provide an opportunity for them to hear other ideas and to sharpen their own thinking.

Alternatively, they could share their frame with two or three other groups or simply write it up as an assignment.

Photographs are an invaluable resource to geography teachers. To make the most of them as a learning resource, it is important to build up skills in observing, analysing and evaluating information from a visual source.

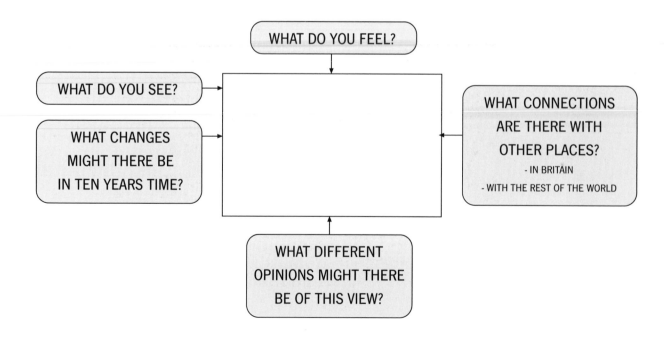

Key questions for 'framing an image'

Activity 2: Now you see it — now you don't

1   Divide the class into pairs and give each pupil a different photograph. Ask them to look at their picture for 30 seconds or so without showing it to their partner. The pictures should then be turned over so they cannot be seen.

2   Pupils should take turns in describing their picture to their partner in as much detail as they can. It is best to do one detail at a time.

3   Each pupil should then turn over their partner's picture that has just been described, look at it, and answer the questions:

   a)   What was left out of the description?
   b)   How is the actual picture different from what was described?
   c)   What things were made up?

Activity 3: What are they doing?

•   Working in pairs, part of the photograph is covered up by one partner. The other is asked to guess the complete picture using evidence such as facial expressions, body positions, dress and the background.

•   Pupils then expose the complete picture, and consider their first reactions to it — how was it different from what they expected?

•   This is an opportunity to point out that **all** pictures are partial, and to highlight the fact that choices have been made about what to include by the photographer, just as the pupils had done in the framing activity.

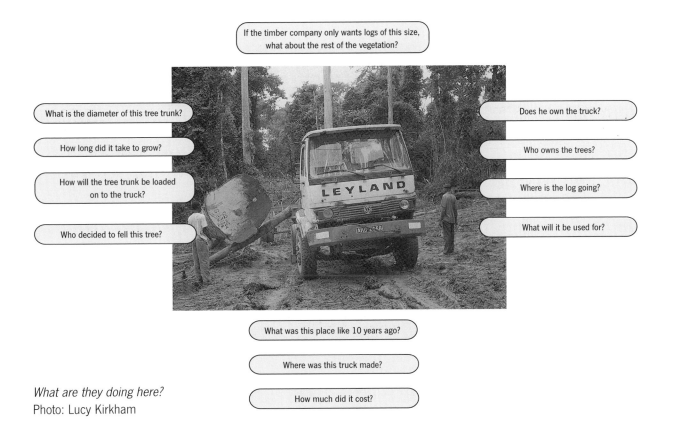

If the timber company only wants logs of this size, what about the rest of the vegetation?

What is the diameter of this tree trunk?

How long did it take to grow?

How will the tree trunk be loaded on to the truck?

Who decided to fell this tree?

Does he own the truck?

Who owns the trees?

Where is the log going?

What will it be used for?

What was this place like 10 years ago?

Where was this truck made?

How much did it cost?

What are they doing here?
Photo: Lucy Kirkham

Activity 4: Questioning a photograph

An activity in which groups focus on just one photograph enables them to take a much closer look at the detail, and encourages them to reflect on the significance of different things shown in the photograph. It also builds up a greater awareness of the limitations of what can be learned from a photograph.

- With three or four pupils per group, give each group a photograph. The ideal is to mount the photograph on a large sheet of paper so that they can write questions around it. Alternatively the questions could be written on a separate sheet of paper.

- Ask them to write as many questions as they can about the photograph. Some of the questions will be very specific and even obvious; others will be rather abstract and occur as a result of discussion about the photograph. Some questions will be almost impossible to answer, but speculation on 'What is s/he thinking?', for example, will help pupils to relate to the photograph and encourage them to identify the wider debates, dilemmas and issues involved.

- Once groups have completed their questions, they can share them either with another group or with the class as a whole.

- You can speed up and also focus the process of sharing these questions by asking them which they felt had raised the most interesting or difficult issues.

The Accra–Kumasi Road
Photo: Scott Sinclair

Borehole well near Obuasi
Photo: Roger Robinson

Activity 5: The Development Compass Rose

The Compass Rose (see pages 12 and 38–39) is certainly one of the most effective tools both for questioning a photo and for developing further enquiry.

There are many other ways in which photographs can be used to explore development.

Activity 6: What do you feel?

This activity can be used with a collection of photographs which you made by, for example, clipping newspapers.

Display a selection of photographs and provide an opportunity for the pupils, working on their own, to take a close look at each one.

- Ask each pupil to select three photographs which they think raise an important issue about development.
- Working in pairs, ask pupils to explain to each other which photographs they have chosen and why. What are the key development issues? Are the issues they have selected similar or different?
- Ask each pair to make a brief report back to the class about the main issues that have emerged from their discussion.
- Ask each pair to choose one photograph which they could use to illustrate a proposal they would like to make for a development initiative. Ask them to prepare a presentation (or make a poster) to highlight the main features of their proposal. These ideas can then be shared with the rest of the class in a way that provides a focus for pupils to express their own opinions, drawing on the things that they have learned.

The Accra–Kumasi road

Perhaps the busiest road in Ghana, this is a main artery for traffic heading north or south carrying people, produce and goods. It is well maintained in most places. State transport provides an efficient service.

- In what different ways does the road system help development?
- What resources are used in transport? Where do they come from and what are the implications for Ghana's need for foreign exchange?
- Are some areas of Ghana better served by roads than others? Why?
- Could Ghana develop a more integrated transport policy involving road, rail and lake transport?

Borehole well near Obuasi, Ghana

The well shown in the photograph is one of over 50 such deep wells provided by the Ashanti Goldfields Corporation in response to claims that their dams and outflow have polluted streams and shallow wells in the area.

- What effects might polluted water have on people living in the area?
- If you were concerned about water pollution near your home, what action might you take?
- When water facilities are being developed, who should be consulted? What concerns might they have?
- To what extent should companies have a responsibility to make good environmental damage that they cause?

Children playing, Birmingham

New Street, Birmingham

Activity 7: Story-boarding

IBT's interactive video *Developing Images* outlines a technique that works equally well with photographs.

Pupils are given a selection of, say, three photographs and are informed that they are stills from a television programme. The task is to write the commentary that they would put with each photo. A time-limit of 10 to 20 seconds may be given.

Two variations of this activity might be to allow the pupils to use the photos in an order of their own choosing or to use them in a fictional account.

The two photos reproduced above are taken from a pack produced by a group of 13–14-year-old pupils. They spent six weeks working in their local area, culminating in their taking over 300 colour photos.

The pupils devised a selection procedure, and produced thirty-five 25 x 20 cm photos. The pupils also produced a set of background notes, and the school now has *The area as we see it* for use with other groups.

Activity 8: A teacher-led photo enquiry

Some knowledge of Nepal and Taiwan is assumed in this example, using photos from Nepal and Taiwan, which could be part of a review or synthesis of work in progress.

Divide the class into groups of about five pupils (or fewer if you have more than one photopack). It is important that pupils sit in positions where they can see and talk to the other members of the group.

Display the photographs and ask each group to select the one they find most interesting. They could mark it with

Nepal: Teaching girls at a literacy class before they spend the day working for their families, Chainpur
Photo: Roger Robinson

Women working in Nepal and Taiwan

It is important that you can see and talk to the others in your group.

1 Your group should choose one photo of Nepal and one of Taiwan to work with.

2 For each photo, discuss the following questions fully in your group.

   a) What economic activities can you see? Make a list.

   b) Have you ever had anything to do with these economic activities? If so, what?

   c) What work are women and girls doing in the photo?

   d) Are there particular reasons for women doing this kind of work?

   e) Could men do this work? Are they doing it? Why is this?

   f) What other people, not in the photo, do you think might be involved in these economic activities? Are they men or women?

   g) Do you think the women in the photo are happy with their part in these economic activities? Explain your thoughts.

   h) In what ways is the work similar to or different from the work most women do in the UK?

3 Compare your answers for the photos from Nepal and from Taiwan. What are the main differences and similarities in the work that women are doing in these particular photos?

Presentation

Fix your photos in the middle of a piece of sugar paper with some blu-tack.

With a felt pen write or draw the results of your discussion on the paper and prepare to make a brief statement to the class about it.

a sticker 'spot' and explain their choice to the class. Use this selection as a basis for providing each group with one photograph of Nepal and one of Taiwan to work on.

Ask the groups to do the exercise **Women working in Nepal and Taiwan**.

Teacher activity

1 Select a photopack to use with a chosen topic/theme/issue being used as a focus for a series of lessons.

2 Plan a sequence of photo activities which would provide an hour's work during this series.

Taiwan: Construction workers in Taidong
Photo: Roger Robinson

Cartoons

The humour that is an essential part of most cartoons appeals to pupils, but the simplicity of cartoons may cause some teachers to overlook their potential. However, cartoons are flexible classroom resources which can be used to stimulate pupils to respond to their content, force them to look at an issue from another's viewpoint, and offer the opportunity to reflect on what has been learned. A good example can be seen on page 50.

Used in a structured manner, cartoons will not only generate and support discussion, but also help pupils observe, analyse and evaluate information, and recognise the value of different interpretations.

What's it got to do with me ... and what can we do about it anyway?

SIGNIE, USA

DE ANGELIS, ITALY

The cartoons on this and the opposite page are reproduced from *Thin Black Lines Rides Again,* DEC (Birmingham)

RAESIDE, CANADA

EWK, SWEDEN

Using cartoons

What's in a theme?
Working in pairs, pupils look at 10 cartoons and group them according to themes or topics. The pupils then share their ideas with other pairs.

Headlining
Working in pairs, pupils are asked to develop a headline and/or short article on the basis of one cartoon.

Reading
Another small-group activity in which pupils concentrate on one cartoon and ask:
*   What is the cartoon saying?
*   Who are the characters?
*   How would other interested parties react?

Matching ...
*   ... cartoons to captions
*   Writing captions to cartoons.

Asking questions
*   Mount a cartoon on a large piece of paper.
*   Working in groups of three or four, pupils write as many questions on the paper as they can relating to the cartoon.

Answering questions
*   Mount a cartoon on a large piece of paper.
*   Surround it with questions, focusing on particular aspects of the issues.
*   Working in groups of three or four, pupils answer as many questions as they can in as many ways as they can.

Chapter 5:
Appropriate
Information

In the same way that a good variety of teaching methods makes for more interesting and stimulating lessons, so the use of different resources is important. This chapter reviews some of the main families of resources, while the Appendix lists some of the resources available.

Starting with immediate sources of information

In conjunction with pupils' own experience, viewpoint and knowledge, it is important to use the real-life resources around them every day as stimuli to their study of geographical issues.

Three suggestions are made here: simple personal mapping of the local area, using objects as stimuli, and the study of newspapers. Each is presented in the context of a lesson activity.

Mapping personal space
Mapping personal space in Nepal
Mobility map drawn by Hira Bahadur Syangtam, an 11-year-old boy from Hayutar, Nepal

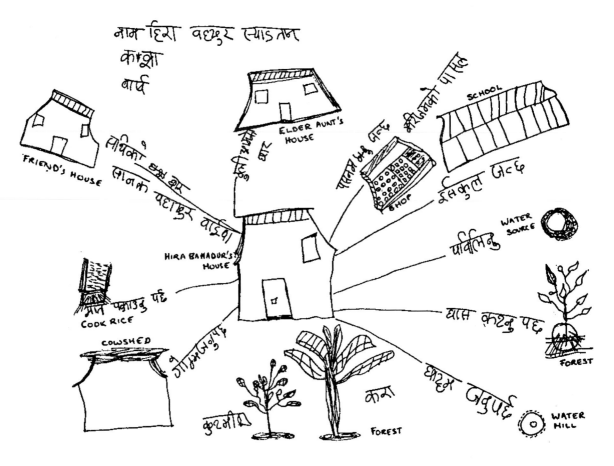

Home area — personal investigation

My activity space

1 Draw a personal mobility map on the outline provided.
Based on your home as the centre, mark and label
all the places you often visit.

2 Join a group and compare maps.
Find the location of each personal map relative to the
centre of your local area.
Discuss the places that several of you visit, and the
places that only one or two of you go to.
Mark the common places on a local map of the area.

3 Write an explanation of who and what decides where
you go and how often you go.

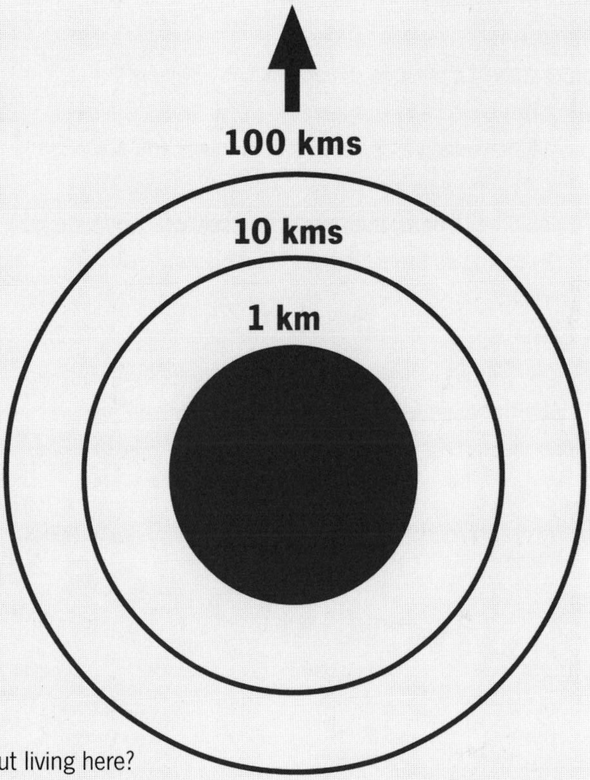

Life in my home area

1 Choose a relative or friend to interview.
Note their background information (age, gender, work
etc.).
Ask them the following questions:
— How long have you lived here?
— What do you think are the good and bad things about living here?
— How has your life changed in the last ten years?
— How have these changes been influenced by changes in your home town?

2 Join a group and compare the recent life experiences.
Note any common kinds of experience.
Suggest reasons for these.

100 kms

10 kms

1 km

Mapping personal space in Britain

Questioning a product

There are many familiar products and items which we
might not immediately recognise as teaching resources,
and yet they may encapsulate a useful range of issues.
Take a can of Nescafé, for example.

• Choose your products. Different groups could have
different ones.

• Working in groups, ask the pupils to examine their
product closely and to discuss the questions
suggested in the diagram.

• Ask each group to decide on three things that are
particularly interesting about their product and which
they would like to share with the rest of the class.

• Have a class discussion about what issues there are
in common between the different products. This might
influence your choice of products if you wish to focus
on particular themes.

Reading into a newspaper

The idea is to use newspaper articles as a source of information, but also to question what viewpoints are being expressed and ask how the pupils see the issues.

1 Make a selection of articles from newspapers which highlight a spectrum of development issues. This could be done by the pupils themselves.

2 Divide the class into groups. Provide each with an article.

3 Ask them to read the article. One person could read, and the others could jot down the main points. Alternatively they could each have a copy of the article.

4 What do they feel about the different viewpoints represented in the article? What viewpoints are missing?

5 Ask the group to share by making a presentation to the class:
   a) what the article was about
   b) what viewpoints they feel are important
   c) what they feel about the issue (do they all agree?)

6 The class could then discuss the issues that arise.

7 They could then go back into the same groups and work together to write their own article from their viewpoint. Remind them about the importance of headlines.

The 'Withers Home' article is a good example of a local development issue in the press.

SHOCK BID FOR WITHERS HOME

A former Sutton Coldfield care home for the elderly, axed by Birmingham social services, may be turned into a home for people with mental disorders.

The proposal, for the Frances Withers home in Avery Road, was criticised by relatives and a leading Sutton councillor.

The home's 29 residents refused to co-operate with social services after it was decided to close the home last year and they stayed put until the very last day.

Places at other homes in the area were eventually found for the pensioners.

On Wednesday the city's social-service committee formally agreed the home was surplus to requirements and that plans submitted by mental-health charity MIND, to turn the home into a residential home for people with mental-health problems, were appropriate.

They now hope to negotiate the sale of Frances Withers to MIND.

Among the proposals is a plan to make 19 beds available for older people with mental-health problems.

Places for five younger people would also be reserved, although MIND has stressed that people with potentially violent disorders such as schizophrenia would not be included in any of the home's places.

Coun. John Hood (Con., Vesey) said: 'I think it should be turned back into an old people's home or turned over to private enterprise.

'I do not think it should be turned into a home for mental patients, because it is in a residential area. I am totally against it.

'There is a shortage of accommodation for elderly people in the Sutton and Erdington area, which has the highest concentration of elderly people in the city.'

Mrs Sheila Fisher, whose 97-year-old mother Ida Kirk was one of the residents moved from Frances Withers, said the proposals did not come as a shock to her.

'We heard rumours about turning the home into different things when were fighting to keep the home open,' she said.

'I think they should have kept it open as a residential home for elderly people in the first place.

'The way in which my mother and the others were thrown out was distressing for all of us.'

Mr David Hart, executive chairman of MIND in Birmingham, said: 'Our aim in this proposed development is to provide a local service for people.

'It is a sad fact that the elderly, particularly those over the age of 85, are at increased risk of developing dementia-type illness and they then require special nursing care which we are very experienced in.

'We intend to work with the residents in the area of Frances Withers and share with them our plans.

'If approval is given we intend to meet them very soon and so develop a broader consultation plan.'

Sutton Coldfield News 13.9.96

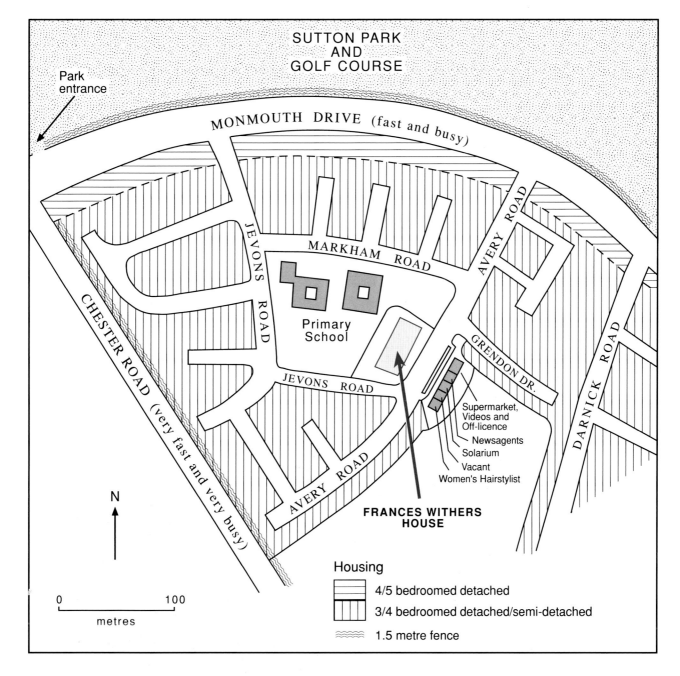

The location of Frances Withers House in Sutton Coldfield

Life histories, cameos, interviews and conversations

Narrative, or storytelling, is probably the most important and interesting way of communicating ideas and information. We use it in conversation every day. Personal stories can be found in cameos and interviews, and these, with short life histories and conversations, can bring to life situations with which the pupils are unfamiliar. This kind of resource is available now in many textbooks, packs and visual materials.

The extract from information about Anloga, the carpentry area in Kumasi, Ghana, gives an example of the use of cameos — short snapshots of people's lives — to

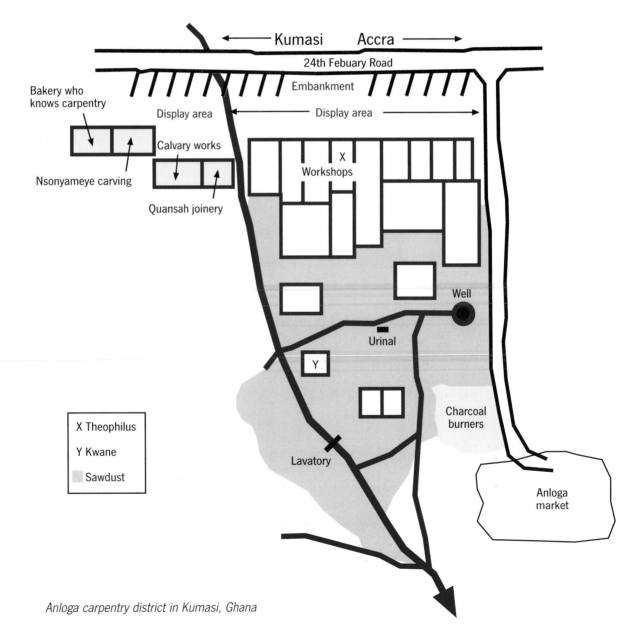

Anloga carpentry district in Kumasi, Ghana

help the pupils to think their way into the issues. Conversation is used to convey information, and provides a personal perspective on development issues.

A short life-history focuses on the time dimension and the changes that occur in people's lifestyle and quality of life as they get older. The history can be presented as a narrative, or as a timeline such as that of Ms Young in Taiwan (page 72).

Cameos from Anloga, Kumasi, Ghana
extracts from *Kumasi and beyond* DEC (Birmingham)

Workshop owner's view
My name is Amevoh. I am the owner of a workshop in Anloga. I was born in Togo and arrived in Kumasi at the age of thirty. There are a lot of other people in Anloga who were born in Togo. We have a strong community and this is very important to us.

If people want to buy something they come to Anloga and walk around. If they like the look of your work and your price is good then they will do business with you. Those of us with workshops away from the main road undercut the prices of people on the main road and most of the customers are aware of this.

There is a lot of waste left over from our work. We give any offcuts to the charcoal seller. We cannot burn any of the waste because of the fire hazard. So we take the sawdust to the river and dump it. This workshop is near to the river so we need to put shavings onto the floor to stop it being swampy.

Theophilus, Manager of 'New Builders Carpenters'
I am from Hohoe in the Volta region and have been in business in Anloga for ten years. We have a good location on the main road which means we sell a lot and because of that we can afford the highest quality hardwood. We mainly make carefully carved doors. We employ twelve people, ten of whom are apprentices, spending five to ten years learning the trade.

Even though we are at the top end of the market in Anloga we still miss out on the very best wood, which goes abroad. I get annoyed about this and I can see a time when we won't be able to get wood as the forests are being felled so quickly.

Kwame, 'Kwami Carpenters'
We are just completing my workshop which we have built with the help of money sent over from my brother in England. It will cost 300 000 cedis [£300] to build. We don't have an ideal location for selling our goods and our plot is so boggy we have to build it up with sawdust, but it means our land is cheaper than others in Anloga.

We are concentrating on tomato boxes and small chairs which we will make from *wawa* – a light-coloured, cheap softer wood. We will employ six workers, four qualified and two apprentices who will be paid 200 cedis [20p] a day. The few tools we have will be imported from Korea and China, we can't afford the more expensive ones from Britain.

Examples of pupil activities
Why do you think so many of the carpenters have travelled such a long way to work in Anloga? Could this explain why apprentices are paid such low wages and kept at that level after they are qualified?

Write a report to the Ghanaian government on the business problems faced by the carpenters of Anloga. It should include:
- the possibility that Ghanaian timber supplies will run out
- the fact that competition means prices are being lowered
- the fact that the price of quality timber is rising
- the problem of the best timber being sent abroad.

Two young students enjoying fast food in a newly opened restaurant in Nantou:

Tom: Does your Dad still want you to work on the farm?

Joe: Yes, but I really want to go to Taipei and follow that business course.

Tom: What are you going to do?

Joe: Well I'm certainly not marrying that girl Christine, just because my family think it's a good idea. My Dad and her Dad were at school together under the Japanese.

Tom: I know what you mean. I'm lucky. This year I'm travelling to Europe to finish my teaching qualifications.

Joe: I would love to do that. Europe is so beautiful and historic. I'd much rather visit Buckingham Palace than the Chiang Kai-shek Memorial in Taipei. I wonder what those guards have under those hats?

Tom: Yes, they have a lot of culture, but they are all out of work and they have forgotten how to make money ... funny, but they don't seem to realise we are catching up fast!

Joe: That's why I want my business qualifications so that I can travel. My parents work very hard but think we should follow their lead and make money no matter what it costs. I do respect them but I wish they would understand what I want.

Tom: When I'm in Europe at least I won't have to listen to my parents all the time.

Joe: Hey, have you heard — a new pizza place is opening in Taichung this week, do you fancy a visit?

Tom: Why not. My motorbike's fixed and I wouldn't mind looking at some new clothes for my trip abroad. Italian would be nice!
So Saturday it is. About 11 o'clock?

Joe: Oh no! I promised my Dad I'd help with the tea harvest. We're up to eight crops a year now, and it's all I seem to do nowadays.

Tom: Well, you can't disobey him — life isn't worth living if you do.

Conversation in Nantou, Taiwan
Extracts from *Can you be different?* DEC (Birmingham)

Born 1962 Taitung. Two older brothers (born 1957 and 1958). Ami aborigine group.

1965 Sister born. Raised in Christian family. Educated up to junior high school standard in aboriginal Taiwanese and Chinese.

1977 Moved to Chung Le to work for dressmaking company. First time she met prejudice, as the majority of those she was in contact with were Chinese.

1982 At evening time went to hairdressing school to gain further education.

1984 Married husband who was a labourer in construction industry.

1985 Older brother died in fishing-vessel accident.

1986 Opened her own shop. People are surprised that she can run a successful business as many Chinese regard aborigines as only spending their money on alcohol.

1988 Boy born, now in kindergarten. They have not noticed any form of prejudice.

1992 She now has 40 customers per day to her well-appointed salon and employs four young girls. She is open from 9 am to 9 pm with two holidays per month.

Her aspirations are to prove the aborigines can run successful business enterprises.

She is a minority Christian in a Taoist and Buddhist society. She is often asked why she does not pay ghost money to the temple and works during the major festivals. She answers that instead she prays for the people for their protection from the ghosts/evil spirits.

Ms Young is a Taiwanese Aborigine working in Taipei

Teacher activity

1 Use the Nantou students' conversation to help pupils think about life in modern Taiwan. Provide suggestions for 'key ideas' that could be given to pupils so that they could search the conversation for evidence of change.

2 Suggest ways in which pupils could compare their own family's life experience with that of someone like Ms Young.

Drama, poetry and novels

Fiction, especially written by authors from abroad, provides real insights into life and environment in other places and cultures. Extracts from novels can help pupils to understand the human dimension of development. Some interesting sources for teachers are suggested in the Appendix.

Poetry too can give an extra dimension to the understanding of places very different from the pupils' own home. Some poems may even have a geographical flavour, such as 'The Motor Under Me Is Running Hot'.

Drama, so seldom used explicitly in geography lessons, can form an important part of simulations when pupils take on roles and improvise in interviews, discussions and decision-making exercises.

Scripted texts, like the conversation in Taiwan, can be acted out by pupils. Scripted plays can be devised by pupils using case-study material as stimulus.

Co-operation with the English/drama department can lead to joint work with benefits for both.

Right: *The Motor Under Me Is Running Hot*
from *An African Prayer Book*, compiled by Desmond Tutu, Hodder and Stoughton, 1996.

Lord,
the motor under me is running hot.
Lord,
there are twenty-eight people
and lots of luggage in the truck.
Underneath are my bad tires.
The brakes are unreliable.
Unfortunately I have no money,
and parts are difficult to get.
Lord,
I did not overload the truck.
Lord,
'Jesus is mine'
is written on the vehicle,
for without him I would not drive a single mile.
The people in the back are relying on me.
They trust me because they see the words.
'Jesus is mine'.
Lord,
I trust you!
First comes the straight road
with little danger,
I can keep my eyes on the women,
children and chickens in the village.
But soon the road begins to turn,
it goes up and down,
it jumps and dances,
this death-road to Kumasi.
Tractors carrying mahogany trunks drive
as if there were no right or left.
Lord,
Kumasi is the temptation
to take more people than we should.
Let's overcome it!
The road to Accra is another problem.
Truck drivers try to beat the record,
although the road is poor
and has many holes
and there are many curves
before we come to the hills.
And finally to Akwasim.
Passing large churches in every village,
I am reminded of you, and in reverence
I take off my hat.
Now downhill in second gear.

Statistics and change

Though statistics seem to be one of the least accessible resources to pupils, they are also one of the most abundant. Teacher sources for development statistics are given in the Appendix. Studies of development can make use of all the standard graphical and diagrammatic techniques to display data, but will place more emphasis on the statistics that show the extent of inequality and the changes in people's well-being. The reliability of the data, what it really means, and what hasn't been measured, become very important in development studies.

Development is particularly concerned with statistics of change and those measuring quality of life.
- Who is doing the counting/measuring?
- What and how are they counting/measuring?
- How reliable are their results?
- What exactly do the measurements mean?
- Does the presentation (e.g. graphs, diagrams) of the data imply a false interpretation?

For indication of change
- What baseline date is used? Was it a peak or trough?
- Are other changes taken into account, e.g. inflation and exchange rates when currency (e.g. US$) is used as a unit of measurement?

For measurement of quality of life
- Are results presented as averages/median values?
- What is the spread of the values?
- Are there other important but unquantifiable indicators?

Teacher activity
Three sets of statistical data are presented in the panels. Take each set separately.
1 Discuss what the data suggests in terms of development. Does anything surprise you?
2 Analyse the strength and weakness of each from the point of view of (a) data (b) presentation (c) underlying assumptions.
3 Develop similar activities for key stage 3 pupils.
4 Suggest a list for key stage 3 pupils to use to check statistical data when they come across it.

	Life expectancy		Infant mortality		Real GDP per capita	
	1960	1992	1960	1992	1960	1992
All developing countries	46.3	63.2	149	70	925	2,595
Least developed countries	38.9	51.4	170	110	592	886
Sub-Saharan Africa	40.1	51.3	165	97	934	1,346
Industrialised countries	na	74.4	na	na	na	15,324

Key

Life expectancy: years at birth

Infant mortality: per 1000 live births

Real GDP per capita: PPP$ (purchasing power parity US dollars)

Development 1960 to 1992
Source: *Human Development Report* 1995

	GNP per capita	Real GDP per capita	HDI
Japan	31,490	20,520	0.937
USA	24,740	23,760	0.937
UK	18,060	17,160	0.916
Chile	3,170	8,410	0.880
Russian Federation	2,340	6,140	0.849
Brazil	2,930	5,240	0.804
Cuba	na	3,412	0.769
Saudi Arabia	na	9,880	0.762
Philippines	850	2,550	0.677
China	490	1,950	0.594
Pakistan	430	2,890	0.483
Ghana	430	2,110	0.482
India	300	1,230	0.439
Bangladesh	220	1,230	0.364
Ethiopia	100	330	0.227
Sierra Leone	150	880	0.221

Key

GNP per capita: US dollars

Real GDP per capita: PPP$ (purchasing power parity US dollars)

HDI: Human Development Index (see page 18)

Economic wealth in selected countries, 1993
Source: *Human Development Report* 1995

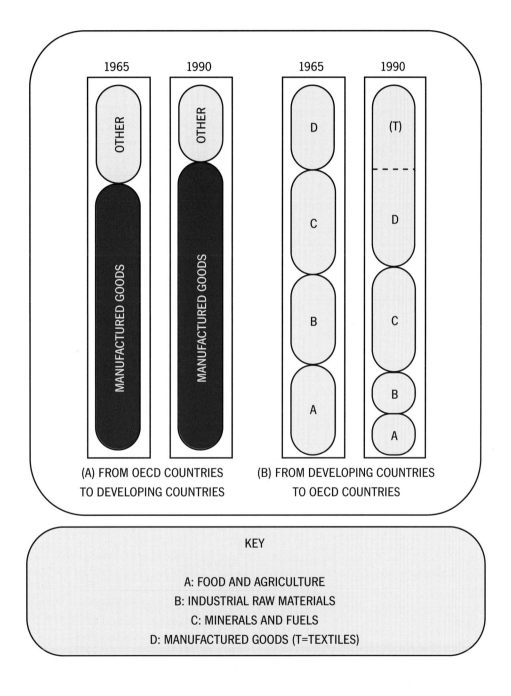

1965   1990   1965   1990

OTHER   OTHER   D   (T)

MANUFACTURED GOODS   MANUFACTURED GOODS   C   D

                         B   C

                         A   B

                                 A

(A) FROM OECD COUNTRIES   (B) FROM DEVELOPING COUNTRIES
TO DEVELOPING COUNTRIES   TO OECD COUNTRIES

KEY

A: FOOD AND AGRICULTURE
B: INDUSTRIAL RAW MATERIALS
C: MINERALS AND FUELS
D: MANUFACTURED GOODS (T=TEXTILES)

Composition of Trade 1965 and 1990
Source: *World Resources* 1994–95

Misconceptions	**Nearer the truth**
1 Development means economic growth and high-technology innovation.	**1** Development has an important economic dimension, but also involves political, social and environmental change and growth.
2 Development can be measured by the proportions of people employed in primary, secondary and tertiary activity — to 'develop', a country moves 'up the scale' towards tertiary.	**2** A total misconception: (a) It ignores the differences of occupations, wealth and conditions within each category. A peasant rice-farmer is classified with an oil magnate and a wheat farmer in the Mid-West of the USA; a São Paulo shoe-shine boy, a bank manager and a hairdresser are all tertiary! (b) It assumes that secondary industrial development is a stage on the way to tertiary. How does being a low-wage exploited factory economy fit in? How did most of the cities of the Third World jump from non-existence to mainly tertiary?
3 The main cause of poverty is too many people in the countries experiencing the poverty. (Blame the victim.)	**3** Another myth which was exploded long since. The UK, the Netherlands and other similar countries are heavily populated but among the richest countries of the world.
4 'Overpopulation' is when the resources of an area cannot support the population living there.	**4** Begs the question of what are the 'resources of an area'. What are the resources of a housing estate in the UK that support a large population? It is a question of having the power and wealth to accumulate and draw in resources. People in many parts of the world with low population densities supply resources to the rest of the world and remain poor — e.g. Ghana, Zambia.
5 A country with draconian birth-control policies is a 'better place' than one without.	**5** While population control can play a part in medium-term economic improvement, it is by no means a development panacea, especially if it is not the result of improved family security, education and living standards. In the long term, what will be the effect in China of a small population of working age and huge numbers of elderly people?
6 Many Third World countries are unpleasant, hopeless places to live.	**6** The negative stereotyping of countries, especially in South Asia and tropical Africa, is based on uninformed acceptance of biased media images and invalid statistical comparisons with the West. Yes, there is dreadful poverty and injustice in many countries, but still 60–80% of the people are not in dire need, and many live fulfilling lives in good conditions.
7 Aid and foreign help are the only way a Third World country can 'develop'.	**7** The minimisation of the part played by Third World people and governments in the development of their own countries is a child of colonialism — both of historical European colonialism and modern financial/cultural neocolonialism. It represents a view from the West which is disproved by the evidence of reality. Maybe, during this period of globalisation, some forms of capital-intensive growth are impossible without foreign capital — but whose development is this about?
8 Third World exports are almost all primary products.	**8** 70% of the exports of Bangladesh, China, India, Pakistan, the Philippines, Sri Lanka, South Africa and Thailand are manufactured goods.

World Development?

Textbooks

Development is certainly the most controversial aspect of school geography, with few 'right answers'. Although there are now many good sets of geography textbooks on the market for key stage 3, we need to be aware of the dangers of over-simplification and the need for pupils to be critical of their textbooks and not to be driven by examination requirements into an 'acceptance' culture. Geography textbooks, even those from the 1990s, must not be taken on trust. Encourage the pupils to look for hidden assumptions and negative stereotypes of people and countries. Watch out for misconceptions and outdated theories.

Occasionally one comes across a textbook in which the approach to development gives real cause for concern. One such is *Interactions* in the *Key Geography* series by David Waugh and Tony Bushell (Thornes, reprinted 1995). In this, the final section on 'World Development' seems to be based on unquestioned assumptions about the nature of development and the causes of poverty. It presents an ill-conceived picture of world development, but in a very accessible and attractive way. The misconceptions listed in the panel are based on *Interactions* pages 84–93.

Chapter 6: From *the Screen*

Videos — moving pictures

The television screen dominates the lives of many of our pupils, appearing to have an almost hypnotic power over some individuals. There is a real danger that it may also dominate our lessons.

The value of the small screen to teachers is immense: it provides vast quantities of up-to-date information in a form that our children find readily accessible, its immediate appeal often generating swift reactions. But this is the danger: **rarely are there opportunities to reflect, evaluate and respond thoughtfully**. Its immediate stimulus generates an immediate response. This knee-jerk reaction is demanded because the programme has already moved on to the next image, comment or point. Its speed forces the viewer into a passive role.

Teachers may also be in danger of being dominated by the medium. Once the video is switched on, one is not encouraged to switch off. The programme takes over, providing images and commentary in a very professional way. The teacher often finds it impossible to add personal comments in the few 'silent' passages, and stopping the tape is discouraged by the programme's continuity and the quietness of the pupils.

If the television screen is to begin to fulfil its educational potential, the pupils must be encouraged to take on an active role. Only then will they question the images they see; only then will they challenge the assumptions behind those images. We teach children to read and think about words and their meanings. We must also teach them to do the same with images.

A worksheet or enquiry activity should always include some questions that can be answered only through what is seen on the screen.

In the following pages, examples are given using the BBC's 'West Africa' series and the *Japan 2000* programmes.

Making good use of the BBC 'West Africa' series

A group of teachers developed this sequence of activities to study *The Tourist Trade*, part 4 of the series.

Activity 1

Having been shown the first two and a half minutes of the film without sound, the pupils are briefed and shown this extract again with sound.

'You have been in Sierra Leone for six days ... what have you seen and done? Write a postcard home.'

Activity 2

When the pupils have seen the whole of *The Tourist Trade*, re-show the first part, freezing about six minutes in at the image shown. The storyboarding activity enables

❏ *Draw sketches and write text to plan continuation of the story on film*

Storyboarding activity
The tourist trade: the story continued

pupils to discuss what might happen. They could, for example, focus on one of the following:

- What happens next?
- What happens when the African family meet later?
- What happens when the tourists meet in the bar?

They complete the storyboard sheet with three more sketches and an outline of dialogue/commentary.

Imaginative education with television

Chris Durbin, in his article in *Teaching Geography* vol. 20, no. 3 (July 1995), provides some excellent advice on the use of televisual resources in geography. The following extracts (pages 79-81) from his comments focus on those most relevant to teaching about development.

What television/video can do well:

- bring distant places to the classroom
- enable people's views to be heard
- explain a difficult concept or process using a combination of images, graphics and commentary
- relate the location of a place to a wider region or even the world, through a set of nesting maps
- demonstrate spatial change in geographical phenomena in graphical form
- bring up-to-date events and topical issues to the fore.

It is difficult for television/video to:

- convey detail on maps
- convey detailed locational knowledge
- convey complex geographical data
- convey subtle and complex viewpoints about an issue
- give you time to dwell on images.

Perceptions

'Perception activities' are widespread in geography classrooms, and they usually begin with a brainstorming session. Unfortunately, if used too often, this can merely encourage pupils to show their ignorance. Using the *Japan 2000* programmes (BBC Education 1994), you could make this process more imaginative. Why not begin by telling your pupils they are on a mystery tour and will be flying in a helicopter over the mystery country?

Ensure you have passed the opening titles, turned down the sound and added a little music to develop the mood. Ask the pupils one simple question: 'Where is this place?' You can be sure they will be watching actively for visual clues. When the programme is over, they can be asked to describe their guesses and to discuss when they knew the country was Japan, what surprised them and what confirmed their perceptions.

Another strategy might be to watch the programme, having been told the place they are going to see, and for pupils to write down adjectives that describe the images seen. Give the pupils time to think after each sequence in order to turn the pictures into words. Selecting adjectives from a teacher-supplied envelope is another useful perception activity.

Rural Japan	Urban Japan
Velvety green +	Lego-like *
Sculpted *	Successful +
Turquoise +	Crowded –
Calm +	Skyscraping *
Crammed –	Vast –
Hilly *	Never-ending –
Narrow *	Dynamic +
Descending *	Polluted –
Totals: +3 –1 *4	**Totals: +2 –4 *2**

In the table above, the symbols denote positive (+), negative (–) and neutral (*) perceptions, as selected by the teacher in question.

Adjectives chosen by one teacher to describe Japan

People

When using television programmes as a resource for teaching and learning about a particular place, cultural and linguistic issues need to be addressed, especially when a programme is made in one country but viewed in others. In Japan, for example, the Confucian philosophy, which underpins parts of the Shinto and Buddhist religions, makes controversial issues difficult to identify. Both sides of an argument (known as Yin and Yang) can be articulated by the same person. This makes teaching controversial issues more difficult, especially if you look at it from a Western European perspective, where adversarial debate is positively encouraged.

In *Japan 2000* programme 1, Mr Nakagawa expresses the view that building a nuclear power station has brought some benefits to his village. The new road has reduced a $5^1/_2$-hour journey to one of only 20 minutes. On the other hand, he recognises the potential danger of the power station, and is also sad that his village has been changed. This exemplifies Yin and Yang.

Name Mr Masua Nakagawa
Age 65
Job Self-employed fisherman
Where he lives Shiraki village, Wakasa Bay, 1 km from a nuclear power station.
Other information Has lived his whole life in the village. He remembers when people died because they could not get to a doctor. His son works in the power station. The new road has brought in visitors who leave their rubbish behind when they leave. It has kept people in the village because they can drive out to work. He is concerned about effects of radiation on his grandchildren and great-grandchildren.

An example of the profiles used in Japan 2000

Developing enquiry skills

Active listening is all-important, and time must be given for pupils to absorb complex viewpoints. The teacher should create the right 'climate' and emphasise the need to *watch*, *pause*, *reflect* and *write* (or discuss). Speech bubbles provide a useful device for pupils to note down information.

Geography is full of unanswered questions, and the use of multimedia interactive technology is a superb way of finding some answers. There are other ways, however. Why not allow the pupils to devise an interview with the Kawamura family featured in *Japan 2000*, programme 3? Tell them they are going to see a programme about a Japanese family and that they must devise a questionnaire.

At present many geography teachers use a question-and-answer sheet for pupils to complete during or after watching a video. These questions are nearly all based on the commentary. Are your pupils encouraged to write down things that relate to the images? Enquiry methods should be used to do just this.

There are fundamental reasons why we need to encourage pupils to enquire actively about any programme they watch:

- The programme is fixed at the time of its production, and it may be being used 1, 2, 3 or even 15 years later. In the case of the BBC *Brazil 2000* programme, for example, Maura, who appeared as a boy, is now approaching 30 and has no idea he is famous.
- The programme was probably made from a Western European cultural perspective.
- The programme may make generalisations that are largely true, but there are always exceptions that are not acknowledged (mostly because of lack of time). In any programme a number of generalisations will be made. Pupils should be helped to identify these and to consider evidence for and against them. They should be encouraged to ask:

- What questions arose from the programme?
- What evidence have I got?
- What evidence do I need from other sources? and where do I find it?

Individual pupils do not have to consider all the generalisations. Instead, the class could be divided into small groups to consider one statement each. If the programme is very out-of-date you may find wide discrepancies in the evidence.

Do not be afraid to challenge your pupils to spot discrepancies and to think about them. One strategy would be to write down a series of true and false statements about things in the programme. Pupils watching and listening to search out the facts are immediately into enquiry mode, asking questions such as 'Where do I find this out?' It may be from the range of textbooks at the back of the classroom, it may be from the library, or it may be from the information in the support materials.

Conclusion

All through this section you have been challenged to think about your strategies for using television/video. 'Active watching' is essential for encouraging media literacy. Actively watching television has four requirements:

- **an inspiring lead-in** to give pupils a clear idea of what they have to do
- **a high-quality environment** in which to watch (big screen, dark room etc.)
- **an active watching** strategy: the tasks or cue sheet should require pupils to interpret the pictures, not just the commentary.
- a clear understanding that they must **watch** the programme as well as **listen** (the pause button can be used to give time for pupils to process the information).

Some videos particularly useful for teaching about development are listed in the Appendix.

CD-ROMs

(This section is adapted from 'What can CD-ROMs do for us?' Fred Martin and Diane Swift, *Teaching Geography*, January 1996, vol. 21, no. 1, pages 20–23.)

CD-ROM (Compact Disk Read-Only Memory) is a digital storage medium using disks identical to audio CDs used in the home. A single CD-ROM can store a vast amount of information — the equivalent of 300 substantial reference books, or hundreds of high-quality colour images. Even this is increasing all the time as compression techniques improve.

CD-ROMs come in many forms, from text-based retrieval systems, which may not be very complex, to multimedia CD-ROMs containing text, graphics, animations, sound and video. Interactive CD-ROMs enable the user to interact with the disk by making choices, and to explore information in either a systematic or a spontaneous way.

There are now many different CD-ROMs on the market. There are pure information sources, such as Microsoft's general encyclopaedia *Encarta*, and a number based on atlases and newspapers that could usefully support development education. There are also interactive CD-ROMs, some of which, such as *Physical World* (published by YITM), cover themes and places, and a few of which focus on particular places, such as *Discover India* (published by Action Aid) and *Kenya: The Final Frontier* (published by Matrix Multimedia).

It is easy to see the potential that CD-ROMs have for development education, but their worth is unproven. They are not yet a regular feature of most classrooms. Now is

the time to explore the teaching and learning priorities that are pertinent to this type of resource.

The more that using CD-ROMs becomes an integral part of a scheme of work, the more likely it is that the pupils will develop familiarity and confidence with the technology.

Rather like the early days of video, there is an initial temptation to see both the teacher and the pupils as passive recipients of this information medium rather than as interactors. The effective use of CD-ROMs should not encourage 'easier' geography, but more demanding enquiry. Outlined below are ten key approaches that relate to development education which could be enhanced by the use of CD-ROMs.

There are issues concerning the cost of both the disks and the computers which cannot be tackled overnight and which need to be discussed within the context of whole-school development. It is difficult to go it alone on this issue, since CD-ROMs have cross-curricular application and pupils will be meeting them in a variety of subjects. However, it is important for the geography department to have a high profile in discussions, since CD-ROMs have an obvious role for enhancing many aspects of our subject, including development.

Do not rush in — a gradual introduction will probably be the most effective!

1 Development education recognises and values the child's own experience of the real world and builds upon it. Many pupils use IT in their social lives and have played geographical games such as SIMCity. We need to build on this, and encourage an appreciation of 'geographical changes' brought about by IT in the world. This needs to be related not only to their own local area but also to distant and global contexts.

2 Development education engages pupils in questioning issues. CD-ROMs can enhance the depth of enquiry, increase the range of information available, and enable pupils to take responsibility for their own geographical enquiries.

3 We have a responsibility to give pupils examples of places in the North and in the South, using high-quality material. Researching contemporary issues, storing the information and devising relevant activities can be enhanced and made easier by the selective use of CD-ROMs. These materials will help to support pupils in making connections between the place being studied and their own locality, while avoiding the problem-oriented approach which can lead to stereotyping and prejudice.

4 The use of CD-ROMs can extend our teaching and learning strategies: they can be used in a variety of ways, both with pupils as independent learners and with teachers using the information. Work using a CD-ROM can either be highly structured or entirely open-ended, or somewhere in between. If the teacher is prepared to relinquish control, the pupils can work through the information at their own pace. This is not without its risks, but the benefits also need to be recognised.

5 The development aspect of a geography teaching scheme should be coherently planned to enable pupils to return to key concepts (e.g. interdependence, justice, power, sustainability). Each of these concepts can be supported by the use of CD-ROMs, allowing the pupils to access information in local as well as distant and global contexts.

6 CD-ROMs can held develop the personal geographies of both teachers and pupils. They give the freedom and flexibility to explore and to go wrong! This can enrich the research process and lead pupils towards a greater understanding of people, places or issues .

7 To explore issues related to development education, pupils should be encouraged to develop skills of critical analysis. Exploration using a CD-ROM should eventually lead to an understanding of an issue at a level which enables the learner to make generalisations and predictions. Too much direction from the teacher may lead to an inappropriate speed of learning, either too fast or too slow for the individual. With too little direction the exploration may fail at the first hurdle, simply because the information is too complex.

8 CD-ROMs (and other computer software) can provide a much broader and more up-to-date information base than many textbooks or atlases. Disks such as *The Times* and *The Guardian* provide information which is updated every six months.

9 CD-ROMs are not a new form of television, ready-made for a quiet lesson! CD-ROMs are tools that can help us to develop our own understanding of concepts and places in a personal and independent way.

10 CD-ROMs are motivating, and can help make geographical development studies enjoyable learning experiences.

Ten reasons for using CD-Roms in development education

'Local-to-global' on the Internet

Development is not something that simply happens elsewhere. It is something that is happening everywhere, regardless of whether a country has been labelled 'developed', 'less developed' or 'developing'.

Pupils need to be given experience of development both in their own local context and in the context of distant localities so that they can make meaningful connections.

A Staffordshire example – the coal-mining issue

A group of Staffordshire teachers have recently responded to this local-to-global challenge. They have been considering issues within their own county and how an enquiry-based approach to learning could be exemplified.

The situation

At the time of writing, there is only one open-cast mine and one deep pit operating within the county. This represents a dramatic decline in coal-mining, with consequences that spread far and wide. Many communities have been affected by the loss of jobs, the reduction in income and the environmental transition that accompany a mine closure. For many pupils within our schools these are real issues: a dad, brother or uncle has quite possibly lost his job, a neighbour may have been evicted because of loss of income, shops and facilities have closed. Many homes still have coal fires, but much of the coal used in Cannock homes now comes from Colombia – a fact that could lead to xenophobia, breeding resentment rather than understanding.

Tackling these issues in classrooms was going to be a challenge. This was made more difficult by the lack of up-to-date materials: most texts still talk of the West Midlands as a traditional mining area. Many of the existing activities were comprehension-style work rather than activities that supported pupils in developing their understanding of the issue.

Information and experience

The teachers felt that there was a need to place the events that had affected Staffordshire in a global context, and to help the pupils see the connections rather than just hunting out the problems.

Initially it was difficult to find out information about the county, but a few individual contacts soon opened doors. The information needed to put Staffordshire in a global context was to be even more problematic. Much of the information was in the form of company accounts or academic reports, often inaccessible to teachers and pupils alike, and frequently inappropriate.

There was then a suggestion that we should 'surf the Internet'. Having heard about several initiatives that utilised the Internet (for ideas relating to the Internet see Durbin 1996) to make global geography accessible to the pupils, a message was left on the American teachers' channel K12, via a friendly local university.

Within hours several usable responses had been posted. One of the most useful was a personal geography from Jeffrey D. Foster, who wrote an open letter talking about the way that the ups and downs of the mining industry in West Virginia, USA, had affected his own personal circumstances.

This resource was perfect for the needs of the Staffordshire teachers. It was personal and accessible, and demonstrated that the booms and busts were not simply something that Staffordshire people experienced, but that these issues were being faced by communities elsewhere. It would help the pupils to consider their own experiences within a wider context.

The teachers then approached a local miner, Jack Sunley, to write a similar personal geography, and the two accounts (reproduced on pages 86–87) together formed the basis of an extremely valuable resource.

Teaching and learning strategies

The pupils needed support to explore their own views and to react in a meaningful way to the information. The activities have been trialled with some Year 8 pupils. Initially the class was split into two halves, one half being given Jack's information and the other half Jeffrey's. They

Michael Baker   3/5/96.

Although Jack and self are
different   they are alike in some
interesting ways.

For example, they both
        worked in the mine

They are also similar in they see Positive and
Negative Sides e.g. Dangerous mines the work is
Both had

The Polution is the same as in camesh is
the same as in america.

The work in camesh resembles the work in the
U.S.A.

Finally, they both
no longer work in mining.

Comparison grid

were asked to read through one of the personal accounts
and to fill in a Compass Rose to summarise the
information that they had found out by reading it. Each
pupil was then paired with someone who had the same
information, and they were asked to fill in their part of the
comparison grid (see illustration).

The pupils were then put into groups of four, two with
Jeffrey's information and two with Jack's. They then filled
in the other half of the comparison grid.

Following this work, the pupils, supported by the
teacher, had a discussion about what they had found out
and about what connections could be made between the
two places. Their thoughts were then summarised on a
writing frame.

This work is part of a much larger project which
attempts to explore the diversity of levels of development
associated with the mining industry.

	Jack Sunley	Jeffrey D Foster
Age/when born	born = 19 January 1925	1953
Where they lived	in a small mining village in Wimbleburg	South West Virginia Tennessee Memphis
A positive effect of mining	get some extra money and coal	Job
A negative effect of mining	Dangerous	Polution through the air
A change that he saw in his local area	that the pits improved from the 1940's onwards	less Job
A change that he saw in the mining industry	It got a lot Safer	Coal best
What does he do now?	He would be retired.	the military

*Writing frame - for more information on writing frames
see pages 112-116*

Hello.

It is my understanding that you are interested in corresponding with individuals that live in a thriving coal industry community. I was born and raised in such a place in the South West part of Virginia. The name of the town was Grundy, and if you look it up on a map it will be rather difficult because the population is only about 4000 people in the whole county.

I was born in 1953 so I had the opportunity to see some of the booms and the busts in that industry. When I graduated from high school in 1969, the coal industry was struggling and most people would get their education and then move to the north where the automobile factories were. I continued my education for the next three years and, in 1972, was in the job market which was a bad time anywhere you went. I went to Tennessee to live with relatives but with no luck of lasting job security. In June of 1973, I made the decision to try the military as a way to get away from the coal industry, as my family knew the perils of the mines and there wasn't work there anyway. Well, I served in the Army until 1976 and, upon returning home, found that the area had changed, mainly due to the oil embargo and the need to ease our reliance on Middle East oil. Where 3 years before I could not buy a job, now I got out of the military one day and next I was working for a coal company as a security guard.

Now when the bust hit, it was like the old saying goes, the further you fall, the more it hurts. Starting in about 1980, the coal mines started to dry up with the environmental protection laws and the fact that coal was harder to find.

It wasn't long before where just days earlier you would be fired for refusing to work overtime, now you were very lucky if you got in a 40 hour work week. At this time, I was driving a coal truck for one of the major producers in the area and had gotten used to the money that I was making because I was working every opportunity I was given and loving it.

The next bust came in November of 1982. At that time, we were doing good and it seems like, in no time, the whole bottom fell out of everything.

In 1985 I decided to go to work for the government as an employee of the Federal Aviation Administration and now I live in a place called Memphis, Tennessee, which is a whole different world. I still live in the South but the environment is so much cleaner here. You don't have the coal dust blowing around all the time and there are not all the dirt roads to travel.

Jeffrey D Foster – a life in mining   *Opposite: Jack Sunley – a life in mining*

I was born on the 19th January 1925 in a small mining village called Wimblebury. Wimblebury Pit was one of some 40 pits in the Cannock Chase coalfield, and in a typical mining village whose employment was 90% mining.

When I started work in 1939 I remember I had to pay the rent arrears on our house, which my father had accrued during the 1926 General Strike. After he died in 1927, there were weeks when my mother could not afford to pay the rent. As a widow, the only income mother had was a state pension of 25 shillings [£1.25]. With this she had to feed and clothe me and my two brothers, and also pay for heat and light.

I passed the Grammar School examination (the 'Eleven Plus'), but my mother could not afford to let me go to Rugeley Grammar School and my place was given to the local chemist's son.

When I left the Central School at 14 years of age, the school sent me for interview at a local colliery office, but I did not like the idea of clerical and office work, so I found my own job at the colliery engineering workshops at Rownsley, then as a surveyor's linesman.

When I arrived home early that day and told mother that I was going to work down the pit, she gave me a good hiding and scolded me because no parent wanted their sons to work down the pit, in dark, dirty, dangerous conditions for poor wages.

I started work down in the Valley Pit on 4th September 1939.

My first day underground at the pit was rather a frightening experience — getting into a metal box like a cage hanging on a wire rope over the shaft which was 1000 feet in depth and was lowered quickly down the mine shaft 1000 feet in 65 seconds in the dark. Living in the mining community, however, I felt I was among friends, mates who would look after me.

I attended evening classes at Cannock Mining College and qualified as a mining engineer (colliery manager), but I had to work below ground for at least 5 years including at least 2 years at the coal face.

I had to wait until I was 18 years old before being allowed to work at the coal face (this was the age for pits in Staffordshire — it varied in other parts of the country). As soon as I was 18 years old, I started to work on the coal face as a 'loader'. This means assisting an experienced miner called a 'stallman'.

I became a pit manager, I had the experience to supervise coal face workers and coal face operations.

From 1947 onwards, all the local pits were improved in the working conditions below ground, the wages of the miners, the environmental aspects as well as the safety aspects. The provision of well-built houses for miners with all mod cons, the provision of social welfare activities, all had to be experienced to be believed. The industry changed from a primitive, uncivilised type of employment requiring hard, physical labour to a technological industry where coal was cut and loaded by machines, using hydraulic trees to support the roof, and remote controlled conveyer systems and locomotives. Haulage systems were introduced.

In the early 1980s, it was felt that coal was not needed as a real source of energy with oil and natural gas being found in plenty and were, apparently, more environmentally friendly. The coal mines began to close down as reserves became less and more restrictions placed on the getting of coal.

The mining industry can be justly proud of the young men who have studied and been helped by NCB to be professional men in electrical and mechanical engineering — men who, through university training offered by the NCB became geologists, scientists, computer experts, college lecturers etc., etc.

Chapter 7: Deeper *Enquiry*

Evaluation and decision-making

It is important for pupils to recognise that information which is presented to them does not necessarily give a true representation of the facts. Information is normally selected to promote a particular viewpoint and designed for a specific purpose. Pupils should be given opportunities to evaluate information.

The skills of evaluation involve:
- careful reading and comprehension
- summarising content
- recognition of the viewpoint from which the information is presented
- recognition of the audience for whom the information is intended
- consideration of the positive and negative implications of the material.

Evaluation is an opportunity for:
- critically examining the material in terms of its assumptions, bias, validity, accuracy and ethnocentricity
- pupils to respond in their own terms
- becoming aware of attitudes to a place or issue.

Activities involving information appraisal by a whole class require careful presentation.

The material must be collected in advance, and multiple copies provided if necessary. This applies particularly to articles and extracts. Space for displaying and viewing leaflets and for discussion may need to be planned.

The teacher should know the background to the information s/he is presenting in order to answer pupils' questions.

It is useful to build up skills in the evaluation of information by introducing activities which draw upon the pupils' knowledge. They should be encouraged to develop an awareness of the extent to which 'facts' are not neutral, but are used within a framework to make a point. Sometimes the same facts, in a different framework, can be used to say very different things.

Facts in the classroom

Pupils can be asked to write down, quite quickly, ten facts, either about themselves — weight, sex, age, etc. — or about their school, their favourite football team, their neighbourhood and so on. Groups of pupils can then compare their lists and consider questions such as:
- Are all the statements accepted as factual?
- Are there differences of opinion over what is,

and what is not, a fact?

- Does a consensus of opinion make a statement fact?
- How easy was it to find ten facts?

Rather than making a list on just one topic, the pupils could be asked to make lists on wider and wider themes: themselves, friends, family, their neighbourhood, their town, their country, the world ... and discuss them in the same way. This activity could also be used to highlight the range of known facts existing in the class. Do their combined statements extend the pupils' knowledge of each other, their neighbourhood and so on? Do the number and variety of facts vary between topics?

Making a point

One way of exploring the ways in which facts can be used to make a point is to try doing just that.

Working in pairs, pupils take a newspaper headline and write stories to accompany it from different points of view — seeing those affected by a disaster as people reaping the consequences of their own thoughtlessness, or as innocent casualties; praising the heroism of rescuers, or commenting on the cost of the rescue operation. How many different stories can they create without inventing new 'facts'?

This could be followed up by looking at the same (real) news story in different newspapers.

- What facts do they agree on?
- What different assumptions do they make?
- What information do they leave out?
- Which account seems (to the pupil) to be the most plausible?

Decision-making work is often the culmination of a place or theme study giving the pupils the chance to use some of the facts and understanding they have acquired. It can also be used to enable pupils to become more closely involved with people and situations if it involves some kind of simulation or role-play.

Who's making the news?
The simple answer is, 'You are'!
Look at the headlines below. They are all linked to farming in Britain in the 1990s.

RECORD HARVEST ... AG(R)AIN!

COUNCIL OF MINISTERS TO LOOK AT FOOD SUBSIDIES

RESULTS OF 'PESTICIDES IN FOOD CHAIN' REPORT PUBLISHED

FISONS: RECORD PROFITS

FARMING RUN-OFF: DANGER TO WATER SUPPLIES?

Select one of the headlines and write the article that you think would appear with it.

But ... write the story as if you were a representative of one of the following groups:

- The National Farmers' Union
- The British Government
- Friends of the Earth
- The Consumers Association

Think ... what viewpoint is the representative likely to have?

You may also like to think about a visual to go with your article — a cartoon (draw it), a photo (sketch it).

Simulating decisions

A central problem in learning about development issues is the degree of complexity often involved. Role-play, simulations and games are good ways of making such issues accessible to pupils.

It is important to be clear about what you are using the simulation for, and then to run the session to support those objectives. There is a danger of seeing the session as a set procedure, a 'party game', with the teacher's role being one of ensuring fair play. It is important to recognise that a good simulation (which is often a simple one) needs to be backed up with other work to provide a context for the results.

Debriefing after the simulation does this, and encourages pupils to reflect on their interactions in terms of the issues explored.

Role-play

Role-play is a technique which allows people to identify with others and to discover new ways of understanding.

It is a useful technique for:

- finding solutions to a conflict/problem
- finding out what it is like to be in someone else's shoes
- building up confidence
- developing communication and listening skills
- preparing for unknown situations such as meeting new people.

Materials are not usually needed, although photographs, stories, newspaper cuttings, cartoons, poems, etc., can all be used as a stimulus to role-play.

Procedure

Choose a specific situation which you want to role-play. Often this will be a spontaneous response to something that has happened in the classroom. Decide how many people are involved in this incident and the roles of those involved. Divide pupils into appropriate groups. Bilingual pupils may want to role-play with friends who speak the same language. Set the scene of the situation by giving

details such as time, place and recent events, or by presenting a problem.

Before the role-play begins, a few valuable minutes can be spent looking at the different characters, each pupil thinking about their character and getting into role. Try to let the role-play work itself through to a natural conclusion, although it may be necessary to set a time limit, as some groups will never come to a satisfactory conclusion.

Follow-up

The debriefing part of the role-play is an integral part of the activity. Various points might be raised, such as what conclusions groups came to, what people in the groups felt at various points, what they think they learned.

Role reversal

To help people look at different sides of the same situation, the role-play can be repeated but with the roles switched. What new insights do you gain from this? Has a different solution been reached? How did the characters feel in the other role?

Freeze

At some point during a role-play the teacher could call 'freeze' and the action stops. This break can be used to ask a question about what the characters are feeling, or for the pupils to discuss what is going on.

Observer

It helps in the debriefing if someone has acted as an observer for a group and can give a more objective view of what has gone on.

Games

Games can provide the high point in a course, and can be integrated into a sequence of learning. Too often they are kept for end-of-term amusement, but as a teacher explains here they can be much more valuable.

Lucy Kirkham, from Bridgnorth Endowed School, reports on two games used in the classroom: The Seasons Game and The Trading Game.

The Seasons Game

The Seasons Game was used as part of a key stage 3 scheme with Ghana as country 'B'.

The games were popular with the pupils and seemed successful in getting ideas across. In some cases games are simply a means of getting pupils to read information as a sequence as they progress by throwing a die. Bad points and good points may be emphasised by allowing players to move on or move back. Often these are not very effective, as the pupils concentrate more on reaching the end and winning than on the information given. There is an example of this type of game in Waugh and Bushell, *Key Geography Interactions*, that aims to show development. I not only take issue with the simplified way in which development is shown as starting in mud huts and finishing in high-rise tower blocks, but also feel that it does not really engage the pupil's interest.

I used a Seasons game set in northern Ghana, from the teacher's guide *Issues and Enquiry* DEC (Birmingham). This is also on a 'throw the die and move' basis, but is not simply a matter of getting to the end. Instead you find your supplies of rice go up and down as you go through the year. It shows the pattern of food surplus and shortage that follows the wet and dry seasons. It also illustrates other aspects of life in northern Ghana, such as the effect of building a well or soil erosion. The pupils enjoyed playing the game, and seemed to appreciate some of the real challenges that the people of northern Ghana face. The first time we used the game we were concerned that the seasonality did not come across as strongly as it should. So, using Paul

Webber's article in *Geography Review* (January 1996) on Zaari village, we modified the game to make sure the player moved from month to month and could not miss part of the year.

The Seasons Game
Introduction

In this game, you are living in Zaari village near Bolgatanga in northern Ghana. You will go through a year or more finding out what activities are done and when they are carried out. You are a subsistence farmer, growing your own food. Your stores of food will change through the year.

Instructions

1 Work in pairs or threes.
2 You will need a 'board' and a die per group.
3 You will *each* need a log sheet and something to write with.
4 Start with 15 bags of food each.
5 Move on *one month* each turn, and throw the die to find out which square to go on:
   a) If you throw a 1 or 2, go to the top square
   b) If you throw a 3 or 4, go to the middle square
   c) If you throw a 5 or 6, go to the bottom square.
6 Keep a log of your progress as shown in the example.
7 If time allows, carry on into a second year, taking whatever food you have with you. *You do not get another 15 bags of food at the start of a new year.*

Year	Month	Event	Outcome	Total store of food
1	Start	—		15
	Jan	sold grain to pay school fees	−2	13
	Feb	sell cattle to buy food	−5	8
	March	start clearing land	+1	9
	April			
	May			

Sample Log Sheet

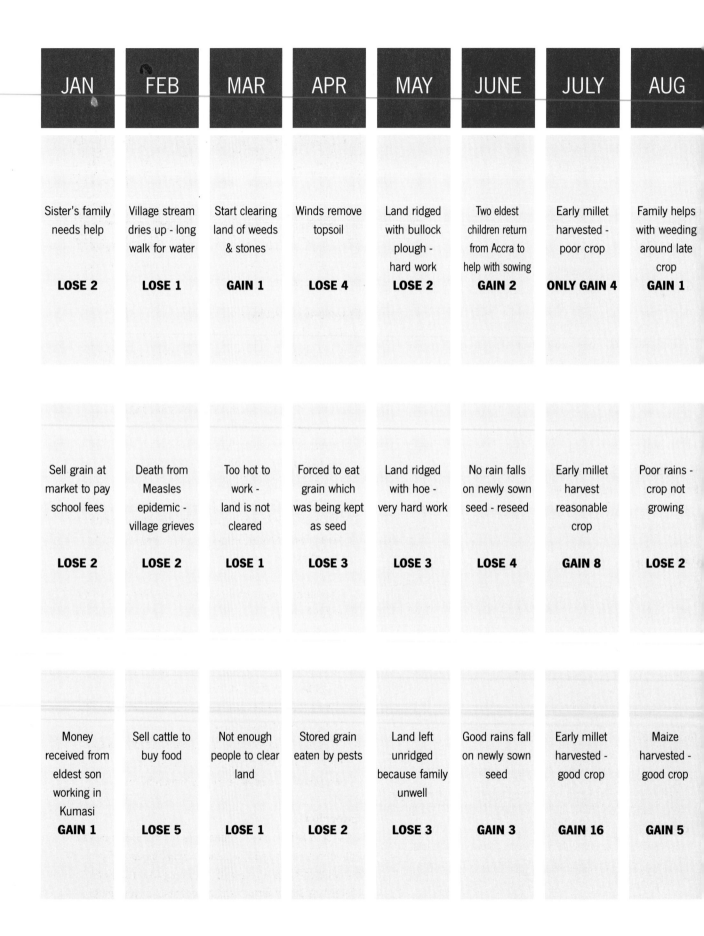

	JAN	FEB	MAR	APR	MAY	JUNE	JULY	AUG
	Sister's family needs help	Village stream dries up - long walk for water	Start clearing land of weeds & stones	Winds remove topsoil	Land ridged with bullock plough - hard work	Two eldest children return from Accra to help with sowing	Early millet harvested - poor crop	Family helps with weeding around late crop
	LOSE 2	**LOSE 1**	**GAIN 1**	**LOSE 4**	**LOSE 2**	**GAIN 2**	**ONLY GAIN 4**	**GAIN 1**
	Sell grain at market to pay school fees	Death from Measles epidemic - village grieves	Too hot to work - land is not cleared	Forced to eat grain which was being kept as seed	Land ridged with hoe - very hard work	No rain falls on newly sown seed - reseed	Early millet harvest reasonable crop	Poor rains - crop not growing
	LOSE 2	**LOSE 2**	**LOSE 1**	**LOSE 3**	**LOSE 3**	**LOSE 4**	**GAIN 8**	**LOSE 2**
	Money received from eldest son working in Kumasi	Sell cattle to buy food	Not enough people to clear land	Stored grain eaten by pests	Land left unridged because family unwell	Good rains fall on newly sown seed	Early millet harvested - good crop	Maize harvested - good crop
	GAIN 1	**LOSE 5**	**LOSE 1**	**LOSE 2**	**LOSE 3**	**GAIN 3**	**GAIN 16**	**GAIN 5**

The Seasons Game board

SEPT	OCT	NOV	DEC
Good harvest of late millet & groundnuts **GAIN 20**	New grain store ready for use **GAIN 5**	Expensive funeral held to honour those who died during the year **LOSE 10**	Expensive party after house building **LOSE 3**
Heavy rains lead to poor harvest **ONLY GAIN 4**	Good harvest of sorghum **GAIN 4**	Chief orders shorter funerals **ONLY LOSE 5**	Women get good price for groundnuts at market **GAIN 3**
Reasonable harvest of cowpeas & rice **GAIN 8**	Good rains - more seeds planted **GAIN 3**	Dowry paid for daughter's marriage **LOSE 5**	Younger members of family travel south to find work **LOSE 2**

North Ghana: drying millet in Apalangu's compound near Bolgatanga. Photo: Jeff Serf

Follow-up activities

1 Draw a line graph showing how your total store of food changed over the year. If you did more than one year, draw the other years on the same graph but in a different colour.

2 Using symbols or labels, mark on your graph when the following occurred:
 a) preparation of the land
 b) sowing of seeds
 c) harvest
 d) food stores at highest level.

3 Use the same horizontal scale as your line graph to draw a bar graph of Zaari's rainfall, using the figures shown below:

4 Look at both your graphs. When was your food supply lowest?
 a) at the beginning of the dry season?
 b) at the end of the dry season?
 c) at the beginning of the wet season?
 d) at the end of the wet season?
 The people call this period 'Houm' which means 'The Hunger'. Mark it on your graph.

5 Using the information in your log and on your graphs, describe how life changes over the year for the villages. You could write this as a monthly diary.

Extension

Draw up a bar graph of Shropshire's rainfall. Describe the differences compared with Zaari's rainfall pattern. Find out what activities are carried out during the year by a Shropshire arable farmer and mark these on your graph.

Month	J	F	M	A	M	J	J	A	S	O	N	D
Rainfall (mm)	0	5	10	50	100	145	170	205	175	50	10	5

The Trading Game

The very best of games and simulations allow players to make decisions that shape the outcome. In this way pupils really begin to empathise with the real decision-makers, and they try to understand the factors which lead to successful decisions.

One game in which the pupils are actively involved in making decisions is the Trading Game. This was devised by Christian Aid, who produce an information booklet on how to play it. Our version is simpler, but it serves to make some important points and has elicited some very thoughtful comments.

The Trading Game

1 Divide your class into three or four groups at tables arranged so that all the members of each group are looking inwards and cannot interfere with any other group. Make sure that all pens, pencils, books, etc., are put away.

2 Explain that each group is a Third World country that needs to earn foreign currency to buy vital things such as hospital equipment, educational resources, food storage facilities and so on. They can earn points (money) by selling paper shapes of specific dimensions that they have to make. The shapes are illustrated here.

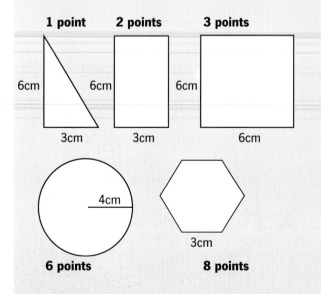

A banker keeps templates which are used to check that the shapes are correct.

3 Each country (group) has only one resource. Give out 12 sheets of paper to one group, 10 pairs of scissors to the second, 12 pencils to the third and 8 rulers to the fourth (or 2 rulers to each group if you only have three groups). Groups can buy a compass for 10 points.

4 Therefore each group has to make a lot of choices:
 a) What to trade for other resources?
 b) How best to make use of the members of the group?
 c) What to produce?

5 Remember that:
 a) Only one person from each group can leave their country (table) at any time.
 b) The prices of the shapes may change if surpluses occur.
 c) Substandard products will be rejected.
 d) Rule-breaking will lead to immediate exclusion from trading.

6 Run the game until the paper supply runs out. Periodically change the price (points value) of the shapes. Well-organised groups will 'play' the market, but most will be caught out.

7 The game works best with an extra teacher or responsible pupil acting as banker, leaving you free to walk round to ascertain the appropriate time to change the prices.

8 At the end of the game, hold a discussion trying to make links with real countries, some of the questions below may help.

9 The pupils can write up the game and answer some of the questions in their books.

Follow-up to the Trading Game

1 What decisions did your group have to make at the start of the trading game?

2 How were those decisions similar to the decisions real countries have to make?

3 During the game your group may have changed how you were working. Describe these changes and explain why the changes were made.

4 When does a real country have to change **what** it produces and **how** it produces them?

5 Anyone who did not stick to the rules was made to sit out and not take part in the trading. How is this like the trade sanctions that were used against Iraq in protest against its internal policies?

6 What difficulties did your group face? Are they like the difficulties a country might face?

7 What happened as your supply of paper got short? Did the way you made your shapes change?

8 How was buying a compass like a Third World country buying machinery from an industrialised country?

9 Were all your group members fully employed, or did you waste this important resource?

Games and simulations do have disadvantages. Reality has to be simplified, and sometimes this is done to such an extent that the game becomes misleading and confuses pupils rather than helping them. However, teachers should accept that simplification can be a strength if, as Walford (1986) wrote, 'it allows dispassionate self-analysis of decisions and observations of total events while working from a particular standpoint.'

1 I got a good deal when I traded the rulers because all the other groups needed a ruler to draw the shapes, we could have done with more than one compass and pencil because the highest points was a circle and more people needed to draw the shapes. Ghana doesn't get a good deal when they trade cocoa because they only get 7 pence out of £1.00.

2 My group got caught out by producing some shapes that were high at the time but when we got around to giving them in the points went down so we tried to make as many different shapes as we could and save them until they got higher points. This is like developing countries because they produce one product and then it can go down in price so they will not make any profit.

3 We got fined for breaking rules just because more than one person kept standing up. This is like Nigeria because they executed a man and most people thought that he was innocent.

Above: Pupils' comments about The Trading Game
Right: Playing the Trading Game
Photo: Lucy Kirkham

Globe Trotting along the West Pacific Rim

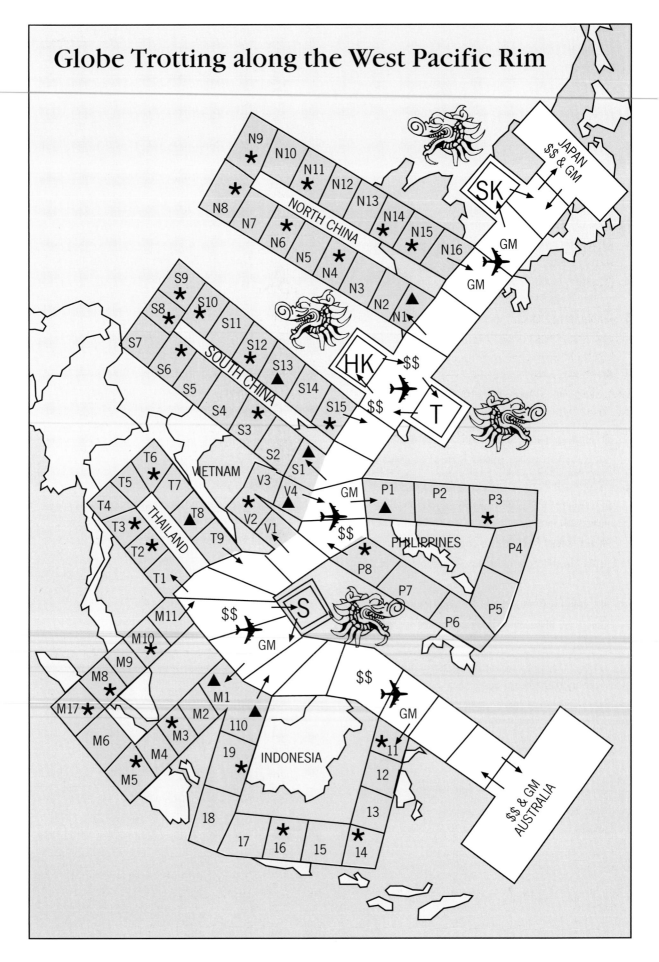

The Four Dragons From *The Global Money Machine*, DEC (Birmingham)

The cards grid (Chance Cards):

Malaysia becomes a core area. Cheap-labour factories there close down, immigrant workers return home.	**North China breaks away from the rest of China. Economy collapses. Factories close down.**	**Hong Kong stock market collapses. HK Dragon will need double global capital, it cannot raise much at home.**
Thailand becomes a core area. Cheap-labour factories there close down, immigrant workers return home.	**Philippines — great political unrest. Civil war, factories close down.**	**Japanese stock market collapses. No more $$ or GM from Japan.**
Indonesia becomes a core area. Cheap-labour factories there close down, immigrant workers return home.	**Global depression. World markets collapse. Value of capital and market units is halved, and everyone moves back 10 squares**	**Vietnam encourages foreign investment. Each factory in Vietnam is worth two units.**
South China becomes a core area. Cheap-labour factories there close down, immigrant workers return home.	**Global boom. Value of market units doubles, and everyone moves on 3 squares.**	**Hong Kong stock market boom. HK Dragon has its own capital available.**

Chance Cards - one per round, shuffled

The Four Dragons

The Four Dragons is another kind of game, trying to simplify the complex working of the global market along the West Pacific Rim.

Globe-trotting along the Pacific Rim

Make up and play a core/periphery game.

A game board is provided — it is based on the West Pacific Rim where the 'four Dragons' of Hong Kong, South Korea, Singapore and Taiwan have become the centre of the world's economic growth in the 1990s. These are now core areas, and look to peripheral areas for cheap labour and land.

In the game each player takes the role of one of the four Dragons. The aim of the game is to collect:

- global capital ($$), i.e. money to invest, from international banks, etc.
- global markets (GM), i.e. to sell your goods world-wide
- migrant workers from peripheral countries to work in your country,
- and to locate factories in peripheral countries.

You can use the following rules and ideas for the game. Having played it through once, you can revise it, or even start again making up your own board or system.

Some suggested rules

1 Four players: the four Dragons (HK, SK, S, T).
2 Start and finish in your own country.
3 You **must** visit Japan and Australia.
4 You can choose to go into other countries when you pass them.
5 Take turns with one die.
6 Keep a record sheet as you go round. On it record where your factories and workers are.
7 Read out one Chance Card at the end of each round until they are all used up. They apply to all players.
8 Global capital ($$) and global markets (GM) can be collected from Japan and Australia, and by flying visits to the USA or Europe when you land on a marked square.
9 When you land on a square marked with an asterisk, you can site a factory and employ local workers.

10 When you land on a square marked with a triangle, you can recruit local workers to go back to your own country.

The rest is up to you.

1 Decide on the detailed aim of your game — for example:

The winner is the first Dragon back home with: 10 factories in peripheral countries, 1 group of migrant labour recruited, 4 units of global capital, and 4 units of global markets.

2 Decide on details, in advance if at all possible. For example:

a) Must you land right on the entry square to visit a country?

b) Must you always go in the same direction until you reach either Japan or Australia?

c) What happens if you land on a rival Dragon?

3 Prepare your record sheet.

Some commercially available games and simulations are listed in the Appendix.

Chapter 8: Teaching Ghana *as Country 'B'*

Lucy Kirkham, Bridgenorth Endowed School

The setting

This chapter is based on a new unit of work that our geography department first taught to Year 9 in 1995, in which country 'B' = Ghana.

I have tried to discuss the process involved in developing the topic, and have included details of the pitfalls we discovered along the way as well as the different aspects that worked well. This should be transferable to other schools and situations.

Owing to pressure on staff time, there is always the dilemma of prioritising, and so certain things are simply not done.

Too often when teaching we make a mental note that this needs changing or that could be added, then before we know it next year has rolled around and we end up hastily filling the most glaring gaps. In the case of the Ghana unit of work, however, we made time to develop a whole new half-term of work. The unit has been successful, and it would be nice to give our whole scheme of work the same treatment. Of course, it will have to be a rolling process and will need to be continually revised. On a positive note, we may become more efficient in developing units of work in this way as we repeat the process.

This is by no means a perfect model, but we hope our experience will help other departments and teachers to identify what decisions need to be made and to see any possible shortcuts.

The department and the school

The school in which this teaching initiative took place is an 11–18 LEA comprehensive with around a thousand pupils. Over a third of the roll come from outside the catchment area. The school enjoys good parental support.

The geography in the school is taught by four specialist geographers, two of whom have other responsibilities in the school. Class size varies between 24 and 30. In key stage 3 there are three one-hour geography lessons in every two-week cycle. Year 7 are taught in mixed-ability groups. The pupils are then setted for all three humanities (geography, history and RE) for the rest of key stage 3. Each year-half has a top set and then two parallel sets below. If the year is too big for this, there are two parallel top sets with two parallel sets below. Some movement between the sets occurs during the years. The school has a Moderate Learning Difficulties Unit. Statemented pupils are taught within mainstream classes, usually helped by a support assistant. Geography is popular at GCSE and A Level.

The need for a new unit in Year 9

Like many schools under the cloud of the National Curriculum, we invested in the ubiquitous *Key Geography* series by David Waugh and Tony Bushell, published by

Stanley Thornes. These books have been criticised, particularly by those lucky enough to be outside the throes of implementing the unwieldy, overloaded and content-prescriptive original National Curriculum. As practising teachers, however, we found them a godsend in maintaining our sanity. The pupils liked them, and we were lucky enough to have class sets for Years 7 and 8. In Year 9 we issue each pupil with their own copy of the book.

Despite the advantages, there are problems in relying too heavily on one resource. Perhaps books should come with something akin to a government health warning, saying 'These books can seriously damage the learning experience if used exclusively.' We are fortunate in having only specialist teachers delivering geography, who had the confidence and experience to add activities and field trips, and to use a variety of other resources.

There was another concern about the books. The clear and straightforward treatment, which in many ways was a positive aspect, did lead to over-simplification in some cases. While we could live with the simplified structure of a volcano, we were more concerned about the basic treatment of development issues. A thoughtful and enquiring approach here is especially important. Our pupils have little multicultural or international under-standing. The ideas they bring with them seem to be gleaned mainly from media images and package holidays.

We had the problem, too, that in both the Year 8 and the Year 9 textbooks, development was left to the end. Initially we followed the order of the topics in the book. Inevitably some earlier units over-ran, leaving the development unit squeezed for time, a problem made worse by the sports day, trips out, exams, SATs and all the other events that go with the summer term.

With the arrival of the revised National Curriculum, which freed up more time and put more emphasis on 'places', we decided that we would write a new unit of work on development to start Year 9. We decided to study one nation in detail to help our pupils begin to get a sense of what life is like in a developing country, and its similarities to and differences from their own lives.

Why Ghana?

1 First-hand knowledge

I had visited Ghana in 1993 on a study visit and had brought back artefacts, slides, etc. More importantly, I had greater confidence in assessing the resources on offer and devising activities, as I felt I was doing this from an informed point of view. This also helped to give the other members of the department more confidence. Just little things, such as knowing how to pronounce a place name, make a big difference.

2 Existing resources

We had taught a little about Ghana in the days before the National Curriculum. We had the 1970s BBC *Ghana* series on video, and we knew it worked well with the classes. Here the first-hand knowledge was of use. We might have dismissed these programmes as being too out-of-date, but my own experience was that many aspects shown on the videos are still very relevant today.

3 Available and affordable new resources

The study visit that I took part in was organised by the DEC in Birmingham who went on to produce two pupil books and a photopack based on Ghana and aimed at key stage 3. These were published in 1995, and we were able to buy a class set of *Land and Life*, one of the pupil books, and two copies of the teachers' pack entitled *Issues and Enquiry* which includes a set of 24 different A4 colour photographs. There are a number of DECs around the UK, and these — along with charities such as Oxfam and ActionAid — produce up-to-date and stimulating resources on developing countries.

4 Ghana's characteristics — a challenge to images

We hoped that Ghana would challenge some of the 'lions, dust and famine' images that our pupils have of Africa. Interdependence is relatively easy to identify, with its colonial past and present exports of cocoa, timber and gold — all very real things in the eyes of a 13-year-old. The marked north/south contrast caused by a variety of physical and human factors helped pupils to understand regional contrasts. Even the shape (rectangular) and size (about the same as Britain) were helpful! Perhaps the most important characteristics were the Ghanaians themselves. We were keen to show the positive aspects of a developing country, and it is easy to relate to the ebullience, humour and commitment of many of the people of Ghana.

Initial aims of the unit

1 To start Year 9 with an interesting and different unit of work

2 To ensure that development is properly covered — it was previously left to the end of the year and often fell victim to over-run of other topics and end-of-year activities

3 To discuss preconceptions and to offer positive images of Ghana

4 To help pupils to realise some of the differences and similarities that they share with Ghanaians

5 To teach about physical and human features that give rise to Ghana's distinctive characteristics and regional contrasts

6 To show how the country is set within the global context and how it is interdependent with other counties

7 To begin to consider ways in which Ghana may be judged to be less or more developed.

Outline scheme of work for Ghana unit

Title	Broad aim	Possible resources/activities	Lessons
Getting There	To orientate pupils to the country and to make them aware of impact of images	Brainstorm word 'Ghana'; quiz; photo activities (page 3 *Issues and Enquiry*); 'African Footsteps' video; world database; atlas work; Ghanaian schoolchildren's perceptions of England (page 5 *Issues and Enquiry*)	1
Features of Ghana and Comparing North and South	To teach about the physical and human features that give rise to Ghana's distinctive characteristics and regional contrasts	North: 'James Obongo' video (page 4 in *Land and Life* updates story); pages 8–17 in *Land and Life*;	4–6
		Seasons game in *Issues and Enquiry* South: 'Cocoa and Timber' video; pages 18–27 in *Land and Life*; 'Volta Dam' video and 'The big project'	
		Overview: Comparing teenagers from North and South; pages 2–3 in Land and Life; map activities pages 6–7 *Land and Life*	
Global Context	To show how Ghana is set within a global context and how it is interdependent with other countries	Trade: pages 28–31 in *Land and Life*; enquiry on pages 12–13 in *Issues and Enquiry*; Trade Game Aid/Assistance: pages 26–27 in *Land and Life* and 'Ways Forward' video; IMF/Structural Adjustment Rummy photocopied from *Kumasi and Beyond*	1–3
Level of Development	To consider ways in which Ghana may be judged to be more or less developed	Compare Ghana indicators with UK and other countries using world database or Population Concern chart figures	1

Ghana classroom Photo: Lucy Kirkham

The process of developing a scheme of work

The concerns described in 'The need for a new unit in Year 9' had been informally raised when the development topics were first taught in Year 8 at the end of the 1992–93 school year, and then again the following year when Year 9 covered development using the *Key Geography* books. Individually, teachers used other resources and activities to improve the quality of the learning. Spurred on by the publication of the revised National Curriculum, it was decided that a new unit of work based on a developing nation was needed. This decision was made in the summer term of the 1994–95 school year.

An outline scheme of work was produced in the summer holidays, as shown in the table.

The unit was designed to last half a term and began in September. All four teachers were involved in teaching the unit; they each developed their own lessons within the outline scheme. Ideas, feedback and resources were exchanged formally at departmental meetings and, more often, informally.

On the Professional Development day after half-term, about two hours were spent discussing the unit and moderating our marking of the written assessment. The scheme of work was rewritten, taking account of these comments and those from the pupils and the Advisor. Only the most successful activities and resources were included in this version. These were described in more detail, and guidance was given to help the teachers to select the most appropriate approach or activity.

The unit is due to be taught again and it will continue to evolve.

Introduction

Pupils should be oriented to the country.

Preconceptions should be discussed, and if appropriate challenged by providing a range of visual information about the country.

Possible activities

1   Brainstorm 'What do you think when I say the word Ghana?' You may need to substitute Africa for Ghana. Keep copy of ideas to refer back to at end of unit.

Follow-up — 5-min clip from *African Footsteps* video — start of second half (Lake Volta, lush, rich, happy)

Pupils write about/discuss/draw what surprised them on the video — 20-30 mins.

2   First half of *African Footsteps* video (15 mins). It may help to introduce video by telling the story:

Once upon a time, about 50 years ago in Ghana, a young boy was checking his family's cocoa trees. It was a serious job looking after trees. When he returned home to his village he was told his father wanted to see him. He was not ready for the news he heard. His father was proud and a little sad when he said, 'The cocoa crop was good. We have enough money to send you to England to go to school and get a good education. You are leaving tonight!'

The young boy went to England and became a successful lawyer. His name was Mr Boateng. He married an Englishwoman and they had a son, Paul. The family returned to Ghana and after it had gained independence from Britain, Mr Boateng became a minister in the new government.

A group of people seized power and put Mr Boateng in prison. Paul and the rest of the family escaped to England. Like his father, Paul became a lawyer and a politician, but Paul stayed in Britain. Paul Boateng is a Labour Member of Parliament. You sometimes see him on the news. Mr Boateng was later released from prison and went back to Tafo, the village where he grew up. Paul now has a son called Ben. Ben is at primary school — a typical London kid — but Paul has always wanted Ben to see Ghana and to meet his grandfather. This film is about Ben's visit to Ghana. Ben's father Paul is speaking.

It may help to stop the video twice to stress the route Elmina (Cape coast) > Accra > Tafo. Suggested stops — after slaves account (end of Elmina) and then after 'famous for cocoa' (start of Tafo).

Follow-up: Pupils imagine they are Ben and write a letter home describing their experiences in Ghana. (Good homework.)

Alternative/additional activities

If pupils are finding it difficult to challenge some of their perceptions, it may help to use Ghanaian school pupils' perceptions of England (*Issues and Enquiry* page 5).

If this video is unavailable, a photopack could be used after the brainstorm — Which photos are of Ghana? What helped you decide? Are you surprised they are all from Ghana?

Take one photo and look closely. What more would you like to know? Write your questions around the photo on an A4 piece of paper.

Notes for Lesson 1 from the revised scheme of work

What does Ghana mean to us at the start of the unit?

Mind map spokes: Africa, Hot, Very little rain, Black people, Island, Poor, Humid, Third World, Shortages, Thundery, Cows, Developing, Snakes, Jungle, Ghana (centre), Tony Yeboah

---

<u>West Watching the Video - What I thought</u>

I was suprised with Ghana because I thorght theit would be no buildings and the would be a stortage of food and water but I thorght it would be in Africa

---

What does Ghana mean to us at the start of the unit?

Morgan F.

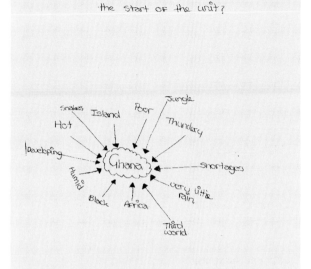

Mind map spokes: Snakes, Island, Poor, Jungle, Hot, Thundery, Developing, Ghana (centre), Shortages, Humid, Black, Africa, very little rain, Third world

<u>Watching the Video - What I thought</u>

Ghana is a very different country from ours what suprised me about the video is that I thought that it would be more Jungle like than it was and also I thought it would be have more shortages than it did. I wasn't suprised by the Hot and Humid climate and also the colour of the people.

Image you are Ben Boatang. write a letter home describe your experiences on your first visit to Ghana.

Dear mum,

The crossing was very good until we came into the port when it got very rough. At once time I did not think we would get there but we did. The port was very crowded with people doing all sorts of different things. we then weat on to a castle where women were locked in and people would walk by and they would be rape a women and if the lady became pregnet and when they did they would be let free. The children were take to a place but most of I died before they got there. I enjoyed going to the castle and seeing all the sights. then we went to a place called Accra where grandad was kept for 3 years I could not a think of what he was going through. After that we went to a place called tafo were my grandad was born and grew up. Tafo is very famous for the cocoa. we walked through a forest and meet grandad and uncle they showe us how to make cocoa. It was finally time to do the thing I was working forward to all day it was time to meet the family. wen we arrived in the little village I saw the builing and I thought about how lucky I am. we got out the car and all the children came rushing towards us. I saw the smile on dads face when we meet the family I could tell that he was

---

Hi Mum,

It's so different than what I imagined here, every thing is so stange. I always thought of Ghana as a dry, dusty place with a short water supply; but I was so wrong the first things I saw from the fisherboat were palm trees and sandy beaches. When we first got into Ghana is was surprisingly windy, I always had an image of it being scorching hot. We found ourselves in a crowded place where the people had simple but colourful clothes and were over-worked. Father pointed out shrines to me that were made for power etc. Our next visit was to a castle near to the port of Elmina. It had once been a place filled/gold until the slave trade started and it became a place filled with slaves. The women were cruely chained to canon balls, the guards then chose a women and raped her. Later if she was found pregnant she would be set free. The children however had to walk on a long journey to be exported, many died before they got there. This information came from a guide.

From there we journeyed to a beach where we saw more black faces, father said there were more white faces some time ago. Then we visited Assha fort where grandfather was imprisoned as a political prisoner. Father described it as a place of sadness and dispair.

We carried on to Tafo where grandfather grew up, he took us straight to see a cocoa plant. This was a fertile place where grandfather's parents found their wealth. The housing was ordinary and then we went to see the school where grandfather was taught, that was ordinary too. The welcome was warm also a bit hard to take seeing all my relatives for the first time. We met a 110 year old man just before father was baptised. Then came the incredibly long welcome called the Akwabe welcoming ceremony, First the elders sit down and the youngers shake hands with them, then the youngers sit down and the elders shake hands with them. After this welcome father gives Tafo (the village) a cheque for over a million cedis(Ghanas currency). Grandfather has to translate what father says into Twi (the language), So the people can understand. They were so thankful. After all of this the people of Tafo dance to strange music played by unfamiliar instruments.
See you soon
from Ben

(A) A very good letter which uses the information from the video which really makes the account convincing

1 Which continent is Ghana in? _____ (1)

2 What is the capital city of Ghana? _____ (1)

3 How big is Ghana?
   a) about the same size as the United Kingdom ☐
   b) about the same size as France ☐
   c) about the same size as Australia ☐ (1)

4 What is Ghana's population?
   a) about four times larger than the UK's population ☐
   b) about the same as the UK's population ☐
   c) about a quarter of the UK's population ☐ (1)

5 What year did Ghana become independent? _____ (1)

6 Which European country held Ghana as a colony? _____ (1)

7 Which of the following could you see in Ghana?

tropical rainforest	☐	elephants	☐
dry grasslands	☐	cattle	☐
dirt tracks	☐	electricity	☐
a motorway	☐	Barclays Bank	☐
mud huts	☐	brick buildings	☐

(5)

8 What is Ghana's currency? _____ (1)

9 What are Ghana's three main exports? Choose from the list:

gold	☐	cars	☐
coffee	☐	cocoa	☐
bananas	☐	coconuts	☐
timber	☐	cloth	☐

(3)

10 What is the link between Ghana and Leeds United Football Club? _____ (1)

11 What is the link between Ghana and Cadbury's? _____ (1)

12 What is the link between Ghana and Body Shop? _____ (1)

13 What is the link between Ghana and
Swan Hattersley Garden Furniture, Telford? _____ (1)

14 What is the name of the lake in Ghana that is one of
the biggest artificial lakes in the world? _____ (1)

Total possible score **20**

Ghana quiz

Aspects of the work

A quiz to start the unit

At the beginning of the unit the pupils were given a quiz on Ghana, and it was stressed that this was **not** a test. We were a little concerned that it might be demotivating as many would fail to get answers to some of the questions. It actually proved to be very successful. Pupils enjoyed researching the answers in a homework, and it got the different classes talking to one another. 'Doing Ghana' became a whole Year 9 thing. It also provided the pupils with a snippet of prior knowledge when we looked at some aspects in detail. This may appear insignificant, but it seemed to make 'primary products' more relevant when most of them remembered the main exports from the quiz. Some of the questions also served to clear up misconceptions.

We also ran the quiz on the school's Open Evening. The pupils had produced display material and mounted photographs from the teacher's pack *Issues and Enquiry* so that all the answers were available to the visitors. It was very successful: over 70 quizzes were completed during the evening, and there was a lot of discussion between the visitors and the Year 9 pupils who had volunteered to run the quiz.

Poems

Pupils watched a video on life in Northern Ghana and were told to write down at least ten describing words. Using these words they then wrote a poem. Surprisingly it worked very well: it encouraged them to absorb the information on the video, and most then found their words enabled them to produce an effective poem. Some examples follow:

Ghana by Rachel
The blistering temperatures and the filthy atmosphere,
Is filled with noise.
The dryness of the day sucks up the oxygen,
Leaving the air dank and heavy.
Few vehicles pass,
Slowly moving towards their destination.
The market swallows up the day,
Leaving only those to pack away.
Some lucky youngster might have found a job,
To provide for their compound.

Poem by Michelle
The atmosphere around me
The music and the noise
People shouting and trading and
Pushing at the market
The rough dusty roads which are
Long when I travel to my school.
Once a week is all I can afford.
This is my life, this is my world
And I enjoy it.

Our City of Hope by Sarah
I walk with my goods to our outside world,
Where the poor exchange their supplies,
But everyone is poor here in the north.
We struggle to feed our young.
Here life equals labour, no luxuries involved.
We all depend on the weather,
Will it be kind this year?
Will our crops grow fine?
We're lucky to have a source of water,
But this is all we have,
The rest is up to us now,
And everything we have is man made.

Poem by Ben
The place that's dusty and hot too,
Has something magical for you.
The place is developing, making things new,
Of which they trade to sell to you.
The schools are few but most people go,
The people want to learn and know.
Any jobs are difficult to find,
No matter how small they wouldn't mind.

Poem by Ben
It can be dry and flat,
Noisy and bare,
Low tech and basic
But we stay there.
We use our resources,
Develop our trade,
Get an education.
WE need the qualifications.
This is Our home
And we're gonna
Stay!

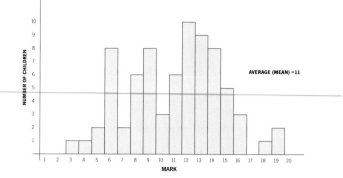

Marks from three classes for the Ghana test

Assessment and evaluation

The assessment played a dual purpose. We wanted to assess each individual's progress and achievement in relation to the aims and objectives of the unit. We also wanted to evaluate how successful the new unit of work had been: whether pupils responded well to the approaches, resources and activities.

It is September 1995 and Year 9 are having their first geography lesson. Those who failed to find the books that they joyfully dumped in July are heaving a sigh of relief: they are told that they do not need their geography exercise books. It had been decided by the department that the pupils would work on A4 sheets of paper for the Ghana unit. These would then be put together to make a folder. We felt this was also an opportunity for some pupils to make a fresh start by working on paper and producing something to be proud of. Each pupil's Ghana booklet was assessed at the end of the unit.

A written assessment under test conditions was also necessary. The school is involved in an assessment scheme known as the Central Record Update (CRU). Twice yearly, subject teachers have to award a CRU level to each pupil; their progress is tracked by comparing their performance with previous years and with the 10+ score achieved at the end of key stage 2. Under-achievers can then be identified and action taken. A scale of 1 to 5 is used to indicate achievement. The figures should also relate to aspects of specified National Curriculum levels. CRU levels for Year 9 were due in the same autumn term as the new Ghana unit. It was the first time for awarding CRU levels, and we wanted a wide range of evidence on which to base our decisions.

Because of the loose nature of the outline scheme of work, the assessment had to enable pupils to show what they knew and understood without being too specific. The test aimed to gauge knowledge of the regional contrasts in Ghana, with the last question being the most challenging and open-ended. It was hoped that all pupils would be able to write something by interpreting the map, but the more able would add more details according to what they

had studied and would be able to show an understanding of the human and physical factors causing the regional contrasts. The assessment was drafted during the autumn term, and the questions and the mark scheme were modified after departmental discussions.

The department carried out some moderation of the marking of the assessment in a meeting and decided on guidelines for awarding the CRU levels. The National Curriculum levels were more difficult as we felt we had not got the feel of the revised levels, so we invited in the LEA Advisor for geography who has a special brief for assessment.

Following these discussions a scheme was set up which involves assessing a limited number of areas in each unit of work. These are to be recorded throughout key stage 3, and then the National Curriculum level will be awarded at the end.

Four areas to be assessed in the Ghana unit were:
1. recording accurately in table form and by using graphical techniques
2. drawing a sketch map
3. observing, recording and analysing information from a video
4. identifying differences between north and south Ghana.

1, 2 and 3 would be assessed using evidence in the pupil's folder. The written test would enable the teacher to assess 4.

The written assessment seemed to work. The test papers were designed to be recyclable to save money, and this could have caused problems for the pupils who find instructions harder to follow if they are not answering by filling in the gaps on the paper itself. However, almost all the pupils managed to complete the test without asking what a question meant or where to write something. When plotted, the marks from three classes (one top set and two mixed-ability, including three pupils with moderate learning difficulties) show a fairly even spread around the mean mark of 11.

1 Look at the map and **write down the letter** which
  shows
  a) the city of Accra _____
  b) the city of Kumasi _____
  c) the city of Tamale _____
  d) Toga _____
  e) Burkina Faso _____
  f) Ivory Coast _____
  g) Lake Volta _____
  h) Atlantic Ocean _____ (4 marks)

2 **Copy and complete** the table using the labels
  below. There is one label for each gap. There are
  three labels for agriculture in both the North and
  South. One label has already been done for you

Few people   Shea nuts   High annual rainfall Timber
Grassland   More people   Long dry season   Cocoa
Rainforest   Coconuts   Rice (with irrigation) Cattle

	North of Ghana	**South of Ghana**
Population	_____	_____
Climate	_____	_____
Vegetation	_____	_____
Agriculture/products: 1)	_____	1) Coconuts
2)	_____	2) _____
3)	_____	3) _____

                              (6 marks)

3 Imagine you were travelling in November from the
  coast to the northern village of Gari along the route
  shown on the map. The whole trip takes three days.
  Each day's journey is shown by a different type of
  line:
  Day 1 ————
  Day 2 xxxxxxx
  Day 3 ···············
  Describe as fully as you can, in the time allowed,
  what you might see on **each day**. Try and explain
  why the scenery, settlements, jobs, farming, etc.
  changes. **You cannot score high marks if you
  just use the information on the sheet.**
                              (10 marks)

Mark scheme for Question 3 of written test
(maximum mark = 10)
1 Follow map and refer to route.   1–2
2 Make simple observations of Ghana's surroundings
  prompted by the map.   3–4
3 Describe some of the features on the route
  using own knowledge to supplement information on
  the map.   5–6
4 Demonstrate awareness of regional contrasts and
  give explanations using own knowledge and
  understanding.   7–8
5 Recognise important characteristics of Ghana and
  describe regional contrasts, giving a detailed
  explanation of why these exist.   9–10

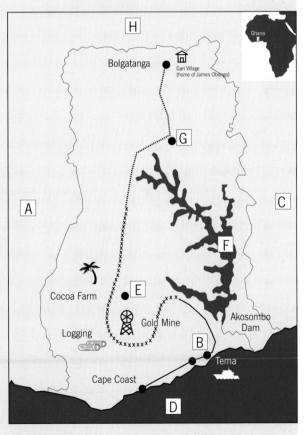

Map of Ghana

Year 9 Ghana Assessment — the test

Pupils' comments on the unit

The folders went only a small way towards evaluating the success of our aim to portray some of the positive aspects of a developing country and to try to balance the many negative images that are shown on the media or assumed through ignorance. About a third of the year group who had completed the Ghana work answered some open questions on the unit at the beginning of the lesson before they started the next topic. The questions were:

1 What did you know about Ghana before September? Very few pupils had heard of the country.

2 How would you describe Ghana to someone who has never heard of it?
This yielded some interesting responses. Some pupils confined their descriptions to factual information that, thankfully, was largely correct ... with the glaring exception of the boy who wrote 'Ghana is in India'.

3 What did you like about the unit on Ghana?

4 What did you dislike?

Scott

Before September I didn't know anything about Ghana. I didn't know where it was or what sort of country it was.

Ghana is a country in the north of Africa. Ghana is split into two types of land, in the north it is dry and there is not much rainfall. The south has more rainfall and there are more big towns there than in the north, there are more roads in the south as well.

In the topic I liked doing most of the things especially the Seasons Game and watching videos.

Shelley

Before September I didn't know anything about Ghana. I learned a lot about it since.

Ghana is a country by the Atlantic Ocean. The rainforest in south Ghana would cover a lot, if it wasn't for human activity, like clearance for roads, logging for timber or collection of fire wood. The north of Ghana is full of dusty roads. School is taken very seriously.

Tom

Before I did this I knew nothing about Ghana, I had heard about it because of Tony Yeboah but I've learned a lot about it now.

Ghana is a small country in Africa. They produce cocoa which is one of their main exports and gold and timber. Tony Yeboah plays for Ghana he has played 19 games and scored 7 goals for his country.

I liked working on paper better than in a book. The videos were good but short.

Abigail

I didn't really know anything about Ghana, I hadn't even heard the name before.

When I first heard about Ghana I thought it was a place that was poor and all scruffy but in fact it looks quite good. They have to make their own houses and they live in round circles of houses. The kids do have to start working young, but not that young about 14–16. They don't have to work long hours but they don't get good pay. They do most of the stuff there themselves like making their own tools and doing their washing in water, they also re-use things if they can.

Lee

I liked —
    working on paper so I could make a booklet
    videos gave us a break from writing
    photo activities were good fun
    Seasons Game because we were able to see what
        real life was really like
    poem was good fun

Some examples of the pupils' comments

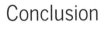

Conclusion

It was interesting to see the different things the pupils commented on favourably. The videos were popular, although some pupils were not convinced by the teacher's assurances that they were still quite true to life and complained they were out of date. The games were also popular, but the rest of the activities were selected by some pupils but not by others. For example, writing a poem was mentioned by five pupils as 'good', by two as 'difficult' or 'boring', and not at all by the rest. It was good to see that everyone had enjoyed at least two things in the unit and that almost every activity had been selected by at least one pupil. Having a range of activities worked well, appealing to the different learning styles of the individuals.

The class books we bought, *Land and Life*, served us well, suggesting a range of activities, although we had to alter some to make them work more easily. Another book in the same series, *Kumasi and Beyond*, focuses on life in a city in Ghana. It would have been better to have both

books, but budget constraints and the number of lessons in the unit led us to purchase only the set of *Land and Life*. Our unit lacks any real urban geography. We accept this omission since the majority of Ghanaians live in rural areas, although the proportion is reducing. We study cities in the developing world, especially Favelas in Brazil, during Year 8. However, we are aware of the vital role of cities in Ghana and draw attention to this during the unit.

Year 9 is a difficult year. Some pupils seem to turn up in September already demotivated. Studying a developing country is apparently 'traditional' geography. However, it gives teachers the opportunity to use a range of resources, and the pupils seem to enjoy learning about somewhere in detail. The Year 9 parents' evening took place more than four months after we had finished the unit of work, yet many parents mentioned that their child had really enjoyed studying Ghana. It was particularly pleasing to discover that the pupils had talked to their parents about it.

Photo activity Photo: Lucy Kirkham

Chapter 9:
In the
Classroom

Teaching the development theme

Aspects of development permeate the whole geography curriculum. Work on any case study or place will give rise to thoughts about lifestyles, quality of life, economic development, and many other dimensions of development. The Matrix of Themes and Scales (page 41) is a reminder that it is often inappropriate to address just one curriculum theme, especially on the human side, to the exclusion of others.

The examples of classroom work in this chapter all have a strong element of development and of development education approaches.

Some teachers who have worked on projects with the DEC (Birmingham) have contributed these examples of classroom work. They offer a spread of content and methods, selected by the teachers from whatever happened to be going on in their lessons when we asked for materials, The brief was to offer something about development involving enquiry with key stage 3.

Youth issues

A report on a photo activity from Tim Thomas at Archbishop Ilsley RC School.
See panel opposite

Taiwan

An evaluation of a photopack by Shaun Lammond at Cardinal Wiseman RC School.
I used a set of photographs of Taiwan from *Can you be different?* DEC (Birmingham) 1994 with a small class of Year 8 pupils with learning difficulties.

The group has behavioural problems in many areas of the school because the work they experience is found by them to be 'boring', uninspiring and often too difficult. They were given one photo each, and I told them that they had to devise a set of questions for their photo. (I showed them how to do this.)

After working individually for 15 minutes, they were then encouraged to help each other think of other questions. The photographs were then mounted on large pieces of card and the questions were printed out by the pupils using a word-processing program. Next lesson, we mounted the questions and displayed the work.

The pupils enjoyed the work and showed great imagination, as the following examples demonstrate: Are they rich? Are they happy? Why is the woman on the lorry? Is she the boss?

I would certainly use the resource again in a similar way.

Part of a scheme of work centred around development and economic activities

1 Teaching aims

- Discussion of youth issues — child labour and links with education
- Key questions:
  How do life experiences of children round the world differ/show similarity?
  Is there a link between poverty and education?
  What rights should children have?

2 Pupil activities

- Working in groups.
- Each group has three photos of children in different parts of the world, e.g. The bicycle shop, photo 12, *Issues and enquiry* DEC (Birmingham) 1995
- Discussion: what economic activities are taking place in these photos?
- Imagine a day in the life of one of the children in the photos.
- Reading: child's life history, e.g. Elizabeth (water seller) in *Kumasi and beyond* DEC (Birmingham) 1995.
- Writing: compare previous perceptions with text; and then with their own lives. Make a list of the comparisons.
- Discussion: should children have rights? — if so, what are they?
- Group presentation to class, then write up in exercise books.

3 Outcomes of the lesson

- Beginning of understanding rights — education, play and leisure.
- Beginning of understanding of the link between poverty and education.
- Beginning of understanding of children's lives in Ghana/Africa.

The bicycle repair shop on a Sunday in a small village near Bolgatanga, northern Ghana
Photo: William Elgar

Loading the village grain crop onto lorries at Yen Ping, Taiwan.
Photo: David Stanton

Key stage 3 Year 9 — band B

Nairobi

A description of several weeks' work with writing frames and photographs, by Diane Swift of Staffordshire LEA

Developing pupils' understanding takes time, and yet that is a key focus of development education. It seemed that, if we followed the National Curriculum in its entirety, then most pupils were going to have a far from satisfactory experience of geography in general and development education in particular. This would affect the less able most, because learning was going to be at an inappropriate pace for them.

Post-Dearing, however, there is more flexibility in terms of teaching and learning. In theory there is less content, although quite rightly there are still arguments about whether or not the content is appropriate. There is also a comparatively freer assessment system, which helps relieve the pressure.

Recently there has been some work published which is not simply concerned with the 'what' of children's learning, but also the 'how'. One of these research projects, the Exeter University Extending Literacy project (EXEL), has developed a structured framework of support for pupils' writing known as 'writing frames', an example of which is shown here. This has been used by a Staffordshire school to support pupils' understanding of the term 'development'. These frames were originally developed for English, but are equally effective with development education.

The following study, on the theme of development, was undertaken by 14-year-old pupils with special educational needs at Alleynes High School, Stone, Staffordshire. The project made use of the *Nairobi* photopack (produced by Action Aid) and took place over half a term (2 x 75 minutes each week). Through it the pupils developed their ability to:

- make use of geographical words or phrases that they didn't know before
- take and record key information from a photograph
- talk/write about development

There are differing explanations as to why (How, what, when, etc.)

One explanation is that _____

The evidence for this is _____

An alternative explanation is _____

This explanation is based on _____

Of the alternative explanations I think the most likely is _____

A blank EXEL writing frame

- describe some differences between a city, a country and a continent
- place Nairobi and Kenya on a map of either Africa or the world.

The pupils were helped to understand that development happens in every country at every scale, and that within each country there is great diversity. We wanted them to understand that both England and Kenya have areas that are developed and developing, i.e. that development is not purely a Third World issue.

To work with these pupils the lessons needed to be carefully structured. Often the pupils are quite capable of expressing themselves orally, and yet when it comes to transferring their ideas to paper they are lacking in confidence. We felt that if the theme were approached in small steps we could develop quite a robust understanding of development. The style of working with the pupils also demonstrated independence, justice and co-operation.

The project made use of the EXEL team's teaching model (see panel).

Teacher modelling
Joint activity
Scaffold activity
Independent activity

EXEL's teaching model

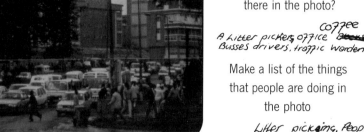

Natural

What is natural about this photo?

Trees with the leaves on.
Puddles of rain on the road.

Who decides?

What clues are there about rules? eg. people driving on the left

• *Tax discs*
• *Traffic Lights*
• *Planning permission for the buildings*

Economic

What job opportunities are there in the photo?

coffee mills,
A Litter pickers office workers
Busses drivers, traffic warden

Make a list of the things that people are doing in the photo

Litter picking, People walking, cars.

Social

Why are there so many people in the street?

Because they are coming home from work. (It's rush hour)

Above and right: Pupil A responds to a photo of Nairobi city centre.

Writing frames are part of the scaffold activity. They help to bridge the gap between joint and independent activities. The prompts in the frames help the pupils to develop their ideas in writing without needing adult supervision all the time.

This was the first time that writing frames had been used by the teachers or the pupils involved in the project. Several features soon became apparent. Initially the pupils needed support and encouragement to write in sentences, as shown by the responses of pupil A. It was suggested to pupils that the frames were there to give them support, so that they could put on paper those thoughts that they often found it easier to say than to write. At this stage their expression of development issues was purely descriptive — the pupils reacted to the stimulus material and wrote what they saw. After about the third session the standard of writing and geographical reasoning improved for almost all the pupils, regardless of their ability within the group. The work (see responses of pupils B and C) shows that they were able to construct more coherent sentences, give reasons and explanations, and use geographical terms appropriately.

The pupils visibly grew in confidence. We found that asking them to read their work out loud helped them to recognise its coherence and complexity. These were pupils that were used to failing at tasks. The open nature of the frames ensured that they were all able to participate effectively, starting at their own level. The repetition of the structure supported their confidence. It was a structure from which they could generalise.

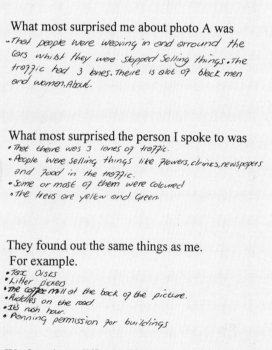

What most surprised me about photo A was
- *That people were weaving in and arround the cars whilst they were stopped selling things. The traffic had 3 lanes. Theire is alot of black men and women. About.*

What most surprised the person I spoke to was
• *That theire was 3 lanes of traffic.*
• *People were selling things like flowers, drinks, newspapers and food in the traffic.*
• *Some or most of them were coloured*
• *The trees are yellow and Green.*

They found out the same things as me.
For example.
• *Tax Discs*
• *Litter pickers*
• *The coffee mill at the back of the picture.*
• *Puddles on the road*
• *It's rush hour.*
• *Planning permission for buildings*

We found out different things.
For example.
The street lights - rules - when you turn them on or turn them off - what time.

They were not being swamped with inappropriate content, but given time to learn. It was noticeable that pupils were staying on task for the full 75 minutes of each session.

When the pupils had used the frames for five or six sessions, a couple of them commented that it was repetitive and boring. By the end of the next week, however, the same pupils were complaining that there was not enough space on the writing frame. The

Images of Nairobi

I was in the group that looked at the photos numbered 2,4,6,9, 11,13

We found the photos interesting for several reasons.
Because it's also simile to England because theire's mosques in Stoke and Longton, esso garages everywhere, theire's a Hotel (the Hyatt regency) next to the international convention centre that has windows like the one in Nairobi and the homes are the same.

We discovered that
~~Everything was written in English.~~

Education is important over theire like in England because you can see Mrs Obard's son and daughter doing homework and in her office all of the work is in english.

We also learnt that
it was very much like England in the way that they have lap top computers and everything is like ours. They call Kenya a developing country and England a developed country but in some ways theire's looks richer than England.

Finally it was very interesting that
A large amount of the population were moslims as we can see in picture 9. The mosque is full of them and theire is 100's outside. So you can see this because the mosque is big.

Pupil B responds to several images of Nairobi.

responses from Pupil C, both on the frame and off it, illustrate a fascinating evaluation made by one of the pupils, and contain some good advice for us as teachers!

Initially many of the pupils thought that the unit was easy, but soon found themselves challenged. The frames helped the pupils to think about priorities, and encouraged them to be critical thinkers, to work collaboratively, to explore justice issues and to consider interdependence — all aspects of development education.

We were pleased with the ways that the pupils responded to photographs of people from a different nation. Through this work they had developed a maturity and confidence which supported them in their approach to development education. We had not expected them to transfer the Compass Rose activity to the second set of photos, which were new to them, without prompting.

One of the key outcomes of this project was the realisation that it is better to consider a relatively small part of the syllabus in depth than to cover large areas without much support. The pupils gained a high level of understanding of the complex issues of development.

Evaluation

Look back at two photo sheets, think about what
you now know about these two places.

Although I already knew that
Nairobi was similar to England because the registeration plates on the cars were English and the name on the factory so they spoke and read English.

I have learnt some new facts
that they (the rich part) has computers and silver in theire houses like england.

I learnt that Some of the goods they produ in Keyna are imported into england like the coffee on the first picture and some of the goods produced in engl are imported in kenya like pottery.

I also learnt that
some of stone is rich and some of stone is poor, and some of Nairobi is rich and some is poor.

Another fact I learnt
was how many people had/hadn't got cars in england.

However the most interesting thing I learnt was that both countries are the same.
Some parts rich and some parts poor.

Pupil C uses a writing frame to evaluate.

I found doing this topic interesting comparing our country to another country. At first i thought the book was boring but after the first couple of lessons it seared getting interesting without the writing frames at the begging i wouldn't be able to write half of the things I did. Now at the end i think (well know) i'd be able to write a writting frame without the writing frames. I thought the book was well easy to understand. But in some of the writing frames i found it hard to fill in the blocks because they asked to many questions like what it felt to be ritch, and the evaluation it says the same question but in different words 5 times! As we got better i felt as though we needed more space in the writting frames as you look in the front you can see i haven't wrote much but on this page you can see i've wrote more. I thought people found this book interesting because it was comparing OUR country to another so we could see how others live. Not just our country our town.

Pupil C responds freely, without a writing frame.

Photos from the Nairobi photo pack
Photos: *Action Aid*

Content/questions	Suggested activities	Resources	Notes/evaluation
What are these places like?	Use Compass Rose to explore Place A (Nairobi, Kenya) and Place B (Stone, Staffordshire). This to be done first individually, then as a class. Summary of class responses on writing frame.	Compass Rose
Photo of Nairobi city centre
Photo of Stone, Staffordshire
Writing frames for photos.
Atlas globe, blank world maps, maps of developed countries.	This will form the pupils' initial reaction and will be referred to at the end as part of the evaluation.
Where are these places? What information do we have about them?	Find places on map. Locate on own world map. Shade 'developed'/'developing' areas on map. Use cards, sort into Kenya, UK and either. Summarise using writing frame.	Information (e.g. GNP, fertility, population) about each place on cards for sorting activity.

Writing frame. | Explore where places are; connect known and distant; make sense of comparisons at country level. |
| How can we measure rich/poor? | Use car ownership as an indicator for the UK. Use IT program to find out about different levels of car ownership at UK, country and town scales. Summarise information on appropriate writing frame. | Pupils were given partially completed maps and asked to finish them using information from the computer. | Different stimulus for writing frames. Activity supports pupils in appreciating that scale makes a difference to how we view development. There are inequalities at every level, which are often generalised. |
| What about Nairobi? | Consider different levels of development in Nairobi. Use ActionAid pack. Class divided into two unequal parts: smaller rich group with more photos, larger poor group with few photos. Work in groups to complete writing frames. | Nairobi photopack, which has images of both the rich and the poor parts of the city.

Writing frame to summarise group findings.

Writing frames to explore the differences between the two groups. | Appreciate variation at local level. Give meaning to the statistics. |
| What did it feel like? | Explore with the pupils what it felt like to be in the rich/poor group. What might this experience help you to understand in both Nairobi and Stone? | Writing frame summary. | Connect personal, local and distant experiences. |
| Evaluation | Explore with pupils what they now understand by the term development, and how this may be different from their views at the start of the project. Explore with the pupils how they learned, what they felt about the writing frames, and about the way in which they were asked to work. | Writing frames. | To ensure that pupils are made aware not only of what they learned but also of how they learned, so that they can transfer these strategies to new contexts. |

Outline of the teaching programme

Migration

Studying UK and Ghana with Year 8 mixed-ability pupils: Helen Potter of Kings Norton Girls' School contributes notes on one lesson and examples of pupils' work.

Pupil activities

1 Where were your grandparents from? Did they migrate?

2 Use an atlas to mark in each person's migration. Label each arrow with their name, and the start and finish of their migration.

3 Sort the migrations (on cards) into 'international', 'internal' and 'both' for each country (Ghana and the UK).

4 Make a list for each country of the reasons why people moved (a) from outside (b) within the country.

5 Compare the lists for each country, are there similarities between the reasons for moving?

6 This example has been about a small group of people. Use the data table for the UK to find out what general patterns of internal migration there are. Find out about the patterns inside another country — say Italy or Brazil.

7 We haven't studied out-migration from the UK and Ghana. What reasons might you have for emigrating? Where would you go?

	IN	OUT	Balance
International Migration			
UK	209 000	213 000	−4000
Internal Migration			
England	99 000	108 000	
Scotland	54 000	47 000	
Wales	52 000	48 000	
Northern Ireland	11 000	12 000	
English Regions			
North	47 000	50 000	
Yorkshire & Humberside	88 000	87 000	
East Midlands	93 000	83 000	
East Anglia	57 000	49 000	
South East	224 000	252 000	
South West	121 000	101 000	
West Midlands	83 000	92 000	
North West	92 000	101 000	

Migration in the UK 1993
Source: *Regional Trends* 1995

Lesson notes

Activity 1: Went through briefly, selecting a few girls at random. The whole class soon started thinking about the topic and migrations their family have made. Very successful.

Activity 2: Went through a few examples, then the girls started. They soon got the hang of it and were well away. Atlas skills were not so good and brought out limitations in geographical knowledge of places. Generally very good. Many were surprised at the scale of movement. They knew it occurs but needed to look at several specific examples for it to sink in.

Activity 3: no problems.

Will be doing Activity 4 tomorrow and drawing some conclusions.

Generally very successful. Will make slight changes with different groups. All abilities were able to cope.

Samuel:

I came to England in 1948 on the very first ship of West Indian emigrants, the Empire Windrush. I was excited and nervous when I arrived. I left Jamaica with my wife and three children as there were no jobs. I had applied for a job as a train driver on the London Underground, who had advertised for workers in Jamaica and offered a cheap passage. However, when I arrived I was offered a ticket collector's job and was disappointed. My family experienced racism and were poorly treated in the early years. We rented a small flat in Wandsworth. My children have grown up and all live and work successfully in London.

Amra:

I came to England as a refugee from Bosnia. I was 11 when I moved here with my mother and older brother. I was saddened to leave Sarajevo, the town in which I grew up. Even worse, I had to leave my father behind. He had become a Muslim soldier in the terrible war that had broken out in former Yugoslavia, the war we had fled from. I now live in Birmingham and have been going to secondary school for three years. I have made many friends and have learned to speak English fluently, but I miss my home country and worry about my father. We hope to return home when the fighting stops.

Jim:

I'm 27 years old. I trained as a teacher in Melbourne, Australia. Unfortunately, teaching jobs were hard to get so I did a variety of jobs just to earn some money. I spent the rest of my time taking part in sports. I earned enough money to start travelling and so headed for America. I then came over to Europe, and ended up in Birmingham. I enrolled with a teaching agency and have been here for over a year and plan to stay until my visa runs out. There are a lot of Australians here and I have also met a lot of other people through sport.

Paul:

I'm 32 and a doctor at University Hospital in Manchester. I trained to be a doctor in Dublin, which is also my home town. Several of my friends came over to England. There were very few jobs coming up in Ireland and competition was strong, so I decided to follow them. I still continue to look for jobs back in Dublin but I am ambitious and in reality I will probably continue my career here. Another influence is that my girlfriend is English.

Margaret:

I retired when I was 60, 16 years ago. I was a teacher. We have lived in Suffolk for 40 years. We have a large number of friends in this area. However, we have to face facts, we are not getting any younger. Our children live in the west of the country, one in Exeter the other near Gloucester. It takes quite a while for them to come over and visit and we have to respect that they have their own lives. We have decided to buy a flat in Weston-Super-Mare so we can be nearer to them. We will be in a milder climate and we will be in a place which has many facilities for people of our generation.

Kamran:

I was educated in Pakistan and studied for a chemistry degree at university in Hyderabad. I moved to Britain when I had finished my degree, in order to look for a job. I felt that there would be greater opportunity to find the type of work that I wanted, and with good pay. I first stayed in Bradford, where I have relatives, and began looking for a job. I was successful within a few weeks and was able to start a well paid job with excellent prospects. The job is with a large chemical factory in Middlesbrough. I have bought a house in Castleton in the North York Moors commute to work every day.

Mary:

I have two teenage children. My husband is a civil servant in London. I am a nurse. We used to live in London when the children were younger. We all had a good social life and generally enjoyed living there. One day my husband had an accident cycling to work. It wasn't bad but it got us thinking. It was a few years after this that we moved to Bath. John still commutes to London each day. I have returned to work in the local hospital. The children have a lot more freedom than they would have had in London. We now have a bigger house with a garden as house prices are lower.

The seven profiles shown on the migration in the UK map (see page 120)

Migration in the UK

Paul:-Dublin to Manchester

Kamran:-Pakistan to Bradford.

Jim:-Australia - America to Birmingham.

Amra:-Bosnia to Birmingham

Samuel:-Jamaica to London

Mary:-London to Bath.

margaret:-Suffolk to Weston-super-mare

Migration in Ghana

Veronica

Burkina Faso → Obuasi

Sheto and Memuna Bawku Kumasi

Amevoh | Togo → Kumasi

Mohammed Abidjan → Kumasi

Elizabeth Bekwai → Kumasi

Ahmed Lebanon → Kumasi

Jane England → Accra

Bawku

Kwaku (18-year-old unemployed man at Obuasi, a gold-mining town in southern Ghana):

I came from Burkina Faso. I want a job with a mining company. They give good money. But too many of us are going for each job. You've got to have a 'friend' inside. Now I'm helping run my friend's private taxi.

Shetu and Memuna:

We are from near Bawku in northern Ghana. We came from a very rural community. Life was very hard in the north so we moved down to Kumasi looking for money and a job. We have become charcoal burners. I have got seven children and Memuna has got eight. The older ones help us with the charcoal burning. Most Ghanaian families use charcoal to light the cookers, so we have a good market for our charcoal.

Amevoh:

I own a carpentry workshop in Anloga, Kumasi. I was born in Togo and arrived here at the age of 30. There are a lot of people in Anloga from Togo, we have a strong community and it is important to us.

Elizabeth:

I left Bekwai, 30 kilometres to the south, a month ago because I needed to make a living. I live with my aunt here in Kumasi, and work selling ice-cold water all day in the market. I hope to raise enough money to buy a sewing machine and train to be a seamstress like my aunt.

Mohammed:

I'm 16 years old and I've been in Kumasi for 2 months. I was born in Abidjan, and I came from the Ivory Coast with my uncle. When he left, I stayed. I work here in the market, carrying people's loads. I've made friends. Some of us sleep in the market, and get up when it gets light. I want to earn enough money to pay for my fare to the coast. There's more jobs there, and they pay better too.

Ahmed:

My family came from the Lebanon thirty years ago. We own and manage a saw mill in Kumasi. We are well settled here, we like the lifestyle and enjoy running a successful business.

Jane:

I work in Accra, the capital. I came from England on a three-year contract as Field Officer for VSO (Voluntary Service Overseas). There are fifty British volunteers in Ghana, I manage their contacts and see to their welfare. I live very comfortably in a large apartment on the outskirts of the city.

Veronica:

I am the community health midwife for a village near to Bawku. I live with my family in the village, and my husband works on a farming project. We came from Cape Coast five years ago.

The eight profiles shown on the migration in Ghana map

Aid and action — political awareness

Claire Dabner of Hillcrest School reports on part of a lesson about aid.

Aid as an aspect of development

The lesson was carried out with a mixed-ability Year 9 class. It was one component of a scheme of work on population and development.

First the class was asked to divide into groups of three or four, and each group was given an envelope with the various 'views on aid' cards. The groups discussed the cards and were then asked to prioritise them, from those they agreed with strongly, down to those they disagreed with strongly. The class then came together and discussed each group's opinions, with explanation.

Next there was a discussion on the types of aid that were available. This was stimulated by a brainstorming session. In the discussion the pupils considered what were the most suitable forms of aid for developing nations.

Again in groups of three or four, the cartoons 'Aid blunders' were distributed, two to each group. These cartoons show various potential problems associated with the traditional forms of aid often given. The groups were given about 10 minutes to discuss them, and they were then asked to present the meaning of their cartoons to the remainder of the class.

A. We shouldn't give Aid- It is only stolen and goes to the rich anyway. It dosn't get to those who need it.

B. Countries need to learn to help themselves. Therefore Britain should give No Aid. Countries should not be dependant upon hand-outs

C. If we give Aid the countries will get richer and will be able to buy o the things that we make.

D. Whats it got to do with us? Its not our problem anyway

E. We should give Aid of some sort. It should go to the people who need it and not the governments who don't use it wisely.

F. Its good to give to countries worse off than ourselves.

G We all live in the same world. We should all help each other.

Views on aid

Aid blunders

Source: *Bangladesh — people and environment*, Christian Aid/Team Video, 1992

Aral Sea — an environmental development disaster

William Elgar at John Willmott School gives an example of Year 9 work.

This example fits in with work on drainage basins and ecosystems as well as development. A variety of information resources were provided, including the cartoons and extracts from *Green Teacher's Resource Book* and several geography textbooks.

The task sheet follows up the viewing of the film *The disappearing sea.*

Aral Sea

Using your film notes, write a news story about the Aral Sea (Disaster)

You must:

1 Design an eye-catching **headline**.

2 Draw a sketch map to show its **location**.

3 Write the story.

Include:

a) The **facts** — what has happened?

b) The **reasons/causes** — why has it happened?

c) How are the local people affected? (a mock interview could be included)

4 Draw a **cartoon** (see examples).

- You can produce a rough draft on paper — cut and paste to decide on the best layout.
- If you have time, word-process using the *Junior Impressions* program.
- You may work with one other pupil on this task, but write your name by each part that you have produced.

Aral Sea pupil tasks

The history of the Aral Sea

22·11·95

The shallow Aral Sea was formally the world's fourth largest body of inland water. It's sometimes called Aral-skoje More. Large saltwater lake straddling the boundary between Kazakistan to the north and Uzbekistan to the South. It nestles in the climatically inhospitable heart of central Asia, to the east of the Caspian Sea. The Aral Sea is of great interest and increasing concern to scientists because of the remarkable shrinkage of it's area and volume in the second half of the 20th century. This change is due to the diversion (for purposes of irrigation) of the riverine waters of the Syr Dar Amu Darya (rivers) which discharge into the and are it's main sources of inflowing water Sea area is characterised by a desert - conti of wide-ranging air temperatures, cold winters, and sparse rainfall. The sea's average -erature for July is 23°-25° C and ice for -mber and December, when the temperature ave F (-0.7 °C). The two rivers which fed the on maps today. The area which was once is now desert with up to 70 million tonnes -t rising into the atmosphere from it - thes -s are sometimes so large they can be space.
The U.S.S.R gets 90 percent of it's white and 40 percent of it's rice from this region. summers, this area is ideal for agriculture very dry, so the land needs to be irrigated fields are watered 10 times a year. Ima -mm of water 5! metres high over each -e of soil - that's how much is used

The Kazakstan Courier

28/11/1995 300rp   Free Television Guide with tomorrows issue!

A Soviet Sea Lies dying!

It has been reported today that by the year 2020 the Aral Skoje, or Sea, will have evaporated down to nothing less than a puddle, if the current shrinkage carries on.

The Government, who approved the building of the cotton farms which use water that would originally have gone to the Aral, didn't think about the devastating consequences it would have on the region. Some of you older readers may remember the Aral in 1970 when it stood at 51 metres above sea level but by 2020 it will be no more than a puddle in proportion to it's original

villages have been put through a devastating chain of events from the dramatic shrinkage of the Amu and Syr Darya in 1980 to this devastating news today. My Governments fore fathers were obviously not thinking about the effect on the nature.
[...] must realise that [...] nature is very [...] anges [...] rom state to state. [...] Nature was [...] it had to be [...] all costs. We need [...] titude before we [...] C.I.S a thriving

Solutions

At present everyone

is sad because of the horrible, nasty Government and Aral sea

But if....... they got rid of the cotton

and used the land

wool

for Sheep which Produce

they would then earn a living

and ...

....they could

Get a huge Ice burg

and ....

let it melt into the empty aral sea re-filling it Then everyone would be happy!

Work by Kathryn, Adam and Michelle

Nuclear power in Japan

Maureen Barwell of Cardinal Newman RC School describes a sequence of four one-hour lessons based on the BBC's *Japan 2000* programmes. These were mixed-ability Year 9 pupils.

Lesson format
Video
Pupils viewed a section of the video 'Against all the odds' (programme 1 of *Japan 2000*). They were shown only the small section near the middle which states that Japan depends on imported energy resources and looks at alternatives to fossil fuels.

I stopped the tape before it investigates nuclear power and the location of power stations at Wakasa Bay.

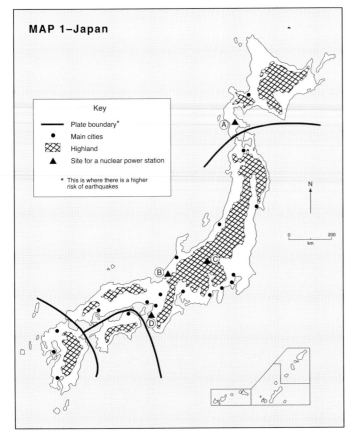

Nuclear power stations must be located:

- On large flat areas of land where there is little or no risk of earthquake.
- Close to water supplies, because a vast amount of water is needed for cooling.
- Away from populated areas, because of safety considerations.
- Not far from the ports where uranium (the raw material) is imported from Canada, France and Australia.

Using the map and other information, choose the best site (A, B, C or D as shown on the map) for a nuclear power station. Give your reasons.

Group work
I had prepared cards beforehand: each card in a set of four had a word related to a particular theme. For example:

Capital cities – Paris, London, Dublin, Athens
Continents – Europe, North America, Africa, Asia
River valleys – river, stream, meander, valley

I gave each pupil one of the cards, and they had to find the three other pupils with related words on their cards. This was a way of getting them into groups of four.

Each group was then given 24 cards with statements about nuclear power.

The pupils sorted the cards into two piles: those statements for nuclear power and those against nuclear power. I checked that the pupils knew what the italicised words mean.

I asked the pupils to prepare an argument for increasing nuclear power from 20% to 50% of Japan's energy requirements. This would involve building more nuclear power stations. (This task could be varied by asking some groups to prepare an argument against nuclear power, or by adapting the cards to provide for less able pupils.)

Four possible sites for nuclear power stations in Japan

Waste from Japanese nuclear power stations is taken by ship to be dumped in France and the UK.

Some people feel that the risk of radiation leaks from nuclear power stations is potentially very dangerous.

Some conservation groups have produced reports which state that the number of children with leukaemia is much higher in areas with nuclear power stations.

The nuclear power station accident at Chernobyl, Ukraine, in 1986 led to many animals being born with genetic defects.

The power stations in Japan use the safest nuclear reactors in the world to produce electricity and the risk of an accident is very low.

Air over Norway was polluted from the nuclear disaster at Chernobyl, Ukraine, in 1986.

Japan has very few *resources* of its own.

Nuclear power is the cheapest way to produce electricity.

80% of Japan's total energy supplies are imported.

The cost of importing the fossil fuels of coal, oil and natural gas is high, whereas the cost of importing uranium is much lower.

Most of Japan's oil comes from the Middle East. The political problems in the Middle East cause concern about this supply of oil, and an alternative such as nuclear power may be preferable.

The world price of oil has increased in recent years.

People who live in a village near Sellafield nuclear reprocessing plant in Cumbria, UK, suffer a cancer rate ten times the national average.

Ravenglass Nature Reserve, near Sellafield nuclear reprocessing plant in Cumbria, UK, is being polluted by radioactive nuclide particles and some bird nesting colonies are disappearing.

Nuclear reactors can produce cheaper electricity. This produces a wide range of benefits, such as:
• the cost to industry is less, so making Japanese goods more competitive in the world market
• the cost to consumers is less, allowing them to spend money on other goods.

Coal mining is a dangerous job. Many miners die of lung disease or are killed in mining accidents.

Some reports suggest that coal-fired power stations themselves emit radioactive waste through their chimneys.

Water from the nuclear power stations is piped into the sea.

Fossil fuels are *non-renewable*. There is already a decrease in the world's oil production.

The risk of *nuclear* accidents worries people.

Nuclear power stations need large amounts of uranium which is imported from France, Canada and Australia.

The burning of *fossil fuels* causes *pollution* (acid rain, greenhouse effect).

As nuclear power stations need large amounts of water for cooling, they have to be built on the coast. In Japan most people live near the coast because it is flat land.

Waste from nuclear power stations is radioactive. The waste has to be stored and disposed of carefully.

Nuclear power 'cards'

I asked the pupils to write down their group's arguments (see the comments from groups A, B, C and D shown on this page and opposite) and then to present them. This could be done orally instead, e.g. as a radio broadcast or a government meeting.

Working individually again, pupils had to choose the best location to build a power station (see worksheet on page 126).

Back to the video

At this point we viewed the rest of the video. This revealed that five power stations were built at Site B (Wakase Bay).

The pupils were asked whether their choice fitted in with Japan's choice, and how people were reassured about the disadvantages of using nuclear power.

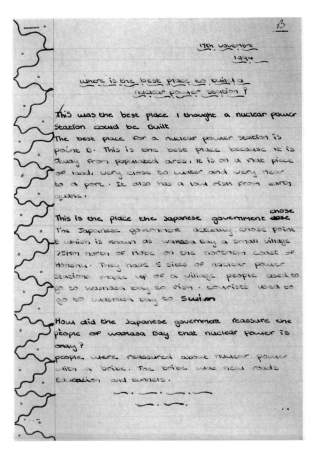

Nuclear power
in Japan

The Nuclear Power stations in Japan use the safest nuclear reactors in the world to produce electricity. Nuclear power is the cheapest way to produce electrcit. Nuclear Power produces cheaper electricity. This makes japanese good's cheaper and so they can sell more good's all over the world. Electricity from Nuclear Power is also cheaper for people's houses. Coal fired power stations emit radio-active waste through their chimneys into the air. There is a big concern about the supply of oil because it is non renewable. But for instant nuclear power can go on for years because it is an renewable source.
The cost of importing fossil fuels is high but the cost of importing uranuim is lower. As years has past the world price of oil has increased. Because the earth is running out and it is a non renewable source of energy. You should use nuclear power because it's cheaper for you and for the producers.
Fossil fuels when burnt cause a large amount of pollution like acid rain the green houe effect and loads of pollution.

Sinneata Johal
Amandeep Paun
Rajieet Ajimal

C

Nuclear Power

"Nuclear energy is a cheaper way of making electricity. People have other worrys about electricity bills, but if they used Nuclear energy it would not cost so much. This produces a wide range of benefits e.g cost to industry is less therefore making Japaneses goods morecompetitive in the world's market and because it costs less and you can spend your money on other goods. Nuclear power stations have to have a lot of water for cooling thats why it is good for Japan because Japan is an island and there are fast flowing rivers. The power stations need people to give electricity to so they can make money and the people need electricity. The power stations are built near to the sea on the coast

When you import coal, oil and natural gas it costs more because the coal and oil is heavy and takes a lot of room and energy to move which means it cost's more. People think that nuclear power stations are very dangerous but in Japan they are new equipment and protection suits to lower the risk of accidents. So nuclear power stations would be the safest and the costs of producing electricity are lower.

Nuclear Power

Japan should have nuclear power because nuclear power is the cheapest way to produce electricity and the price of oil is increasing as it is running out.
Even though, radioactive waste is produced it is not such a problem in Japan, as they have the safest reactor in the world and they dump their waste in Europe.
The fact that Japan has very few sources of energy means that 80% of their energy supplies are imported.
People say that working with nuclear power is danger but working in coal mines is equally as dangerous. The coal mines can produce radioactive waste as well.
Fossil fuels could be used but burning them causes pollution especially acid rain and greenhouse effect. They are more expensive to import than uranium.
Nuclear power may be dangerous but finding a perfect resource that doesn't damage the environment and peoples health is impossible e.g nuclear power is just as good if not better than

Land is valuable in Japan. Here two paragliders fly over the outskirts of a huge industrial conurbation on Kyushu
Photo: Noel Whittall

Kenya

Lisa James of Cockshut Hill School shares the results of using the BBC's _Zig Zag_ programme with Year 9 pupils.

The programme I used, _Zig Zag,_ contrasted daily life in Kenya for two young schoolgirls.

- Nana lives in a rural area, her family farm the land and her father lives and works in Mombasa.
- Evangeline lives in an affluent part of the city of Nairobi, has professional parents and attends a good school.

The video contrasts their lives with those of English children, drawing out similarities and differences in development.

Life as a young Kenyan

Nana is a rich kenyan, Evangaline is a poor and Adam is a normal English boy

6:00am Nana gets up, gets washed puts on h uniform, she then either has fruit, fru porridge or cereal.

6:00am Evangaline wakes up, gets washed ar dressed and has tea and fried eggs feeds the calf.

7:00am Adam gets dressed and has a wash, having cereal maybe toast or a big

7:30am Evangaline leaves for school on foo passing many fields

7:45am Nana leaves for school in car and a forest.

8:15am Adam leaves for school with a choir or in car to arrive at school.

During school

Nana when at school sings the na anthem with their flag rose.
At dinner time Nana can bring her lur provided by the school.

Evangaline sings the national anthe but in the school yard. Her school u and is very tatty.

Adam has an assembly in a school At dinner time he can either bring his buy some food or be provided by th

6:00pm Evangaline collects water and does th
Nana does her homework and wat

Adam plays out with his mates, also his homework and watches t.v.

Life as a young Kenyan

Adam Jones.   6th June 96.

Life in Nairobi

Evangeline is a girl who lives in Kenya She wakes up at
6:00 of a morning, She has her breakfast tea with fried eggs.
Then she feeds the carve Sometimes the carve does'nt let go
of it's food.

She goes to School at 7:30 She walks because it's Not far
the School, She lives with her Mam and dad because the other kids
are at boarding School.

Her School is like a Shed with four to a desk their are squac
hed up together, after School She does homework then dances
because their live in a poorer Country of Kenya than others So
there don't have a tele. Evangeline is different from us of a
night She dances because there's no tele to watch and of
a Morning She goes to school early than us.

But in a Similar way She does homework and goes to sch
ool

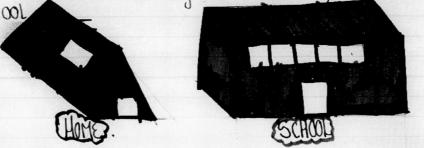

HOME.   SCHOOL

Nani is the Same Sort of person? She Wakes up at 6:30 She
get's dressed then has breakfast She has fruit Juice if it's cold
She has porigge. Nani goes to school in the car to school becau
se She likes for to walk, She passes a little forest then
She gets to School at 7:45, When the bell goes She lines up
for Assembely then She sings the national Anthem as the flag
is being raised. When the bell goes at 12:00 She goes to launch
English is the Lesson it is 1 to a desk, when the bell goes
at 4:00 it is Hometime.

Life in Nairobi

Chapter 10:
In Conclusion – *the National Curriculum and the International Charter*

This handbook has shown how geography and development education can work hand in hand to provide key stage 3 pupils with the opportunity of an open, enquiring and balanced understanding of the changing world. Together they will do far more than they can individually

There are some aspects of geographical education that we have not stressed, not because they are unimportant but because they are not the central concern of this relationship. You will find them discussed in the GA's secondary Geography Teachers' Handbook .

The concepts and content of development and development education are particularly relevant to the teaching of Country 'B' and to the themes of ecosystem, population, settlement and economic activities, as well as development. The approaches and methods encouraged by development education closely match the key stage 3 geography skills.

Geographical education has a central role to play in the education of pupils for an active and informed citizenship. The following extracts from the IGU *International Charter on Geographical Education make* clear the importance and potential of the partnership between geographical and development education.

International Charter on Geographical Education

This *International Charter* was endorsed by the International Geographical Union in 1992 and first published in 21 languages in 1994. It was published in full in *Teaching Geography* April 1995.

The following extracts are particularly relevant to the work of geography and development education in partnership.

Preface

The Commission on Geographical Education of the International Geographical Union is:

Convinced that geographical education is indispensable to the development of responsible and active citizens in the present and future world.

Conscious that geographical education can be an informing, enabling and stimulating subject at all levels in education, and contributes to a lifelong enjoyment and understanding of our world.

Aware that students require increasing international competence in order to ensure effective co-operation on a broad range of economic, political, cultural and environmental issues in a shrinking world.

Challenges and responses

The resolution of major issues and problems facing our world requires the full commitment of people of all generations. All of the following issues have a strong geographical dimension:

population dynamics, food and hunger, urbanisation, socio-economic disparities, illiteracy, poverty, unemployment, refugees and stateless persons, violation of human rights, disease, crime, gender inequalities, migration, extinction of plants and animals, deforestation, soil erosion, desertification, natural disasters, toxic and nuclear waste, climatic change, atmospheric pollution, water pollution, ozone holes, limits of resources, limits to growth, land use, ethnic conflict, war, regionalism, nationalism and globalisation on 'Spaceship Earth'.

The conflicts created by these problems and issues present a challenge to geographical educators who are committed to giving all people the hope, confidence and ability to work for a better world.

Skills in:

- using verbal, quantitative and symbolic data forms such as text, pictures, graphs, tables, diagrams and maps
- practising such methods as field observation and mapping, interviewing people, interpreting secondary resources and applying statistics
- using communication, thinking, practical and social skills to explore geographical topics at a range of scales from local to international.

Such a process of inquiry will encourage students to:

- identify questions and issues
- collect and structure information
- process data
- interpret data
- evaluate data
- develop generalisations
- make judgements
- make decisions
- solve problems
- work co-operatively in team situations
- behave consistently with declared attitudes.

Attitudes and values conducive to:

- interest in their surroundings and in the variety of natural and human characteristics on the surface of the earth
- appreciation of the beauty of the physical world, on the one hand, and of the different living conditions of people, on the other
- concern for the quality and planning of the environment and human habitat for future generations
- understanding the significance of attitudes and values in decision-making
- readiness to use geographical knowledge and skills adequately and responsibly in private, professional and public life
- respect for the rights of all people to equality
- dedication to seeking solutions to local, regional, national and international problems on the basis of the *Universal Declaration of Human Rights*.

In particular, geographical education promotes understanding, tolerance and friendship among all nations, racial and religious groups and furthers the activities of the United Nations for the maintenance of peace by actively encouraging:

a) an international dimension and a global perspective in the education of people at all levels

b) understanding and respect for all peoples, their cultures, civilisations, values and ways of life, including domestic ethnic cultures and cultures of other nations

c) awareness of the increasing global interdependence of peoples and nations

d) ability to communicate with others

e) awareness not only of the rights but also of the duties incumbent upon individuals, social groups and nations towards each other

f) understanding of the necessity for international solidarity and co-operation

g) readiness on the part of the individual to participate in solving the problems of their communities, their countries and the world at large.

Content and concepts of geographical education

In their studies, children should be encouraged to adopt a questioning or enquiry approach which will lead them towards the statement and application of generalisations and principles.

Issue-based approaches are concerned with the study of current issues and problems from a geographical point of view. These may be at local, regional, national or global scales.

Choice of approach

The preferred educational philosophy determines whether the above approaches are combined or whether one only is selected. Whichever approach is adopted, studies should encourage students to engage in questioning and enquiry. It is essential that students develop the geographical skills of seeking solutions to current and future problems in the organisation of space. In this way, geography curricula play a substantial role within political, social, ethical, personal, humanistic, aesthetic and environmental education.

National Curriculum Geography – Key Stage 3

The National Curriculum Geography Programme of study is conceptualised within a framework that gives great importance to the understanding of development and issues in the real world. The ideas and suggestions in this handbook are strongly reflected in the Programme of Study.

Global to local

Case studies
Personal histories

Core/periphery
Development
Globalisation

Change
Justice
Equality

Interdependence

Preparation >
inquiry > synthesis

Local development
issues

Discussion
Presentation

Development
processes

Interviews
Mapping

Foreign maps
Maps of localities

Geography
Key Stage 3

KEY STAGE 3 PROGRAMME OF STUDY

■ **1.** Pupils should be given opportunities to:

a investigate places and themes across the whole range of scales;

b undertake studies that focus on geographical questions, *eg 'What / where is it?', 'What is it like?', 'How did it get like this?', 'How and why is it changing?', 'What are the implications?',* and that involve fieldwork and classroom activities; studies should involve the development of skills, and the development of knowledge and understanding about places and themes;

c explain geographical patterns, and physical and human processes;

d consider the issues that arise from people's interaction with their environments;

e become aware of the global context within which places are set, how they are interdependent, and how they may be affected by processes operating at different scales, *eg how a locality is affected by a regional economic policy or a world trade agreement.*

GEOGRAPHICAL SKILLS

■ **2.** In investigating places and themes, pupils should be given opportunities to:

a identify geographical questions and issues and establish an appropriate sequence of investigation;

b identify the evidence required and collect, record and present it;

c analyse and evaluate the evidence, draw conclusions and communicate findings.

■ **3.** Pupils should be taught to:

a use an extended geographical vocabulary, *eg ecosystem, drainage basin, tertiary industry, sustainable development,* to explain geographical patterns and change, and to investigate relationships;

b undertake fieldwork, selecting and using appropriate techniques and instruments to measure and record accurately, *eg land use survey, data logging;*

c make maps and plans at a variety of scales, using symbols, keys and scales, *eg an annotated sketch map showing key features drawn from an OS map;*

d use and interpret maps and plans at a variety of scales, including Ordnance Survey 1:25,000 and 1:50,000 maps, the work should include using six-figure grid references, following routes, identifying relief and landscape features, drawing cross-sections, and using maps in decision-making exercises;

Pupils should be taught to:

e make effective use of globes and atlases to find appropriate information, and to locate places studied, places that are in the news, and the points of reference specified on Maps D, E and F (pages 15–17);

f select and use appropriate graphical techniques to present evidence on maps and diagrams, *eg pie charts, choropleth maps;*

g select and use secondary sources of evidence – photographs (including vertical and oblique aerial photographs), satellite images and other sources, *eg census data, visits to school by representatives of local interest groups* – to inform their studies;

h use IT to gain access to additional information sources and to assist in handling, presenting and analysing geographical evidence, *eg automatic weather stations to collect weather data, spreadsheets to record environmental impact scores, CD-ROMs to obtain census data, desktop publishing packages to produce a leaflet on a local issue, simulation packages to investigate a flood hazard.*

PLACES

■ **4.** Two countries, other than those in the **United Kingdom**, should be studied. They should be in significantly different states of development. One country should be selected from the areas in LIST A, the other from those in LIST B.

LIST A	LIST B
Australia and New Zealand	Africa
Europe	Asia (excluding Japan)
Japan	South and Central America
North America	(including the Caribbean)
Russian Federation	

Geography Key Stage 3

■ **5.** For each of the two countries, pupils should be taught:

a about the physical and human features that give rise to the country's distinctive characteristics and regional variety;

b about the characteristics of two regions of the country and their similarities and differences;

c about the ways in which the country may be judged to be more or less developed;

d how the country is set within a global context and how it is interdependent with other countries.

THEMATIC STUDIES

■ **6.** The nine geographical themes below should be investigated. These may be taught separately, in combination with other themes, or as part of the studies of places. Whichever approach is followed, thematic studies should be set within the context of actual places and some should have topical significance. Taken together, the studies should involve work at local, regional, national, international and global scales, and provide coverage of different parts of the world and different types of environments. Contexts should include the local area, the United Kingdom, the European Union and parts of the world in various states of development.

GNP, GDP, Real GDP, HDI, GDI.

Present development data

Photographs Television Interviews

Development Compass Rose

CD-ROMs

Presentation of individual and group inquiry work

Change and development processes

Detailed study Personalised local case studies

What is development? Dimensions of development

Globalisation Interdependence What happens to people? What should happen?

Appendix: Resources

This list of resources provides an idea of the materials available today, but is by no means exhaustive.

Development education classroom resources

Cities — a better life?
An activity pack for key stage 3 geography
CWDE (now Worldaware) 1992
Case studies of the problems faced by people living in urban areas in Brazil, Mexico and the UK. It looks at differences and similarities, and makes links with pupils' own experiences.

Colonialism, conflict and community
Cross-curricular themes in the classroom
DEC (Birmingham) and Trocaire 1993
Ideas for teaching about communities in change, based on Birmingham, Dublin and São Paulo; how conflict has affected people's lives in Belfast and Cambodia; and the effects of colonialism on Ireland and South America, from the perspective of both coloniser and colonised.

Focus on Ghana
Water and development issues
Severn Trent Water and DEC (Birmingham) 1995
Explores the factors which influence access to safe drinking water, using case studies from the Severn and the Volta. Includes background information and photocopiable activity sheets.

Food matters
The question of food in the world
DEC (Birmingham) and Trocaire 1992
This pupils' textbook raises many issues about hunger and poverty. It considers food as a basic need and a human right, and looks at what caused famine in Ethiopia.

'Developing geography: Ghana' series

DEC (Birmingham) 1995

Issues and Enquiry: teaching about a nation

A teachers' pack to use with the two pupils' books below. It offers ideas for planning and teaching about a nation state, avoiding biased and stereotypical images. The photopack has sections on youth, international links, economic activity and justice, gender, and the environment. Backed up with case study material from Ghana.

Kumasi and Beyond: urban development and enterprise

A textbook for pupils about Kumasi, a regional city in Ghana. Colour photographs introduce pupils to the city and its people. Their personal stories and the supporting activities explore urban and regional development.

Land and Life: rural development and primary production

A textbook introducing pupils to Ghana, its people and regional variations. The drier north of the country is contrasted with the rainforests of the south. Village life, farming, trade in gold and cocoa and possible paths for further development are all explored, using colour photographs, maps and activities.

Planning to teach about development issues

DEC (Birmingham) 1995

This handbook is the result of a series of workshops with teachers from the Ghana Geographical Association. Its main aim is to stimulate further creative work in Ghana but the approaches to planning have a wider application.

'It's our world too!'

A local–global approach to environmental education at key stages 2 and 3
DEC (Birmingham) 1992

What do we mean by sustainable development? How do we achieve it? These are two of the issues addressed in this teachers' handbook. It offers practical activities to help explore the issues, and strategies for planning work on local–global issues.

Kenya — a geography resource pack

Worldaware 1995

Information and activities on Kenya with sections on population, trade, aid and debt.

Mapping our world

Oxfam 1993

Provides a variety of world maps and activities for pupils to question the purposes and use of maps.

Market trading

A simulation game
Christian Aid 1992

Explores the likely impact of the European Single Market on less prosperous countries outside the EU.

Namaste India pack

Worldaware 1995

A pack containing classroom sets of country information sheets and mapcards plus photocopiable units on topics such as trade, aid and development and population issues.

The coffee chain game

An activity on trade for participants aged 14 years and upwards
Oxfam 1994

A role-play putting players in the position of people involved in the coffee trade, from growers in Uganda to supermarket managers in the UK.

The global money machine
Resources and ideas for a wider understanding of the global economy and 'core/periphery' patterns – for key stages 3 and 4
DEC (Birmingham) 1994
Taiwan is the focus for examining economic development and asking what happens when new rich nations emerge. Activities, games and case studies bring the issues to life.

The chocolate game
Leeds DEC 1995
A simulation game looking at the cocoa trade in Brazil, Ghana and the UK, and how chocolate production affects people's lives.

'Southern perspectives on development' series
Manchester DEP 1996
1 **Starting points:** the power of words and images, what is development, the creation of poverty, interdependence.
2 **Colonialism and its legacy:** the South before colonialism, European expansion, social and economic impacts, independence and neocolonialism.
3 **Distribution of people and resources:** levels of consumption, food, health, population.
4 **Production and its effects:** work, the transnational economy, migration and urbanisation, technology and sustainability.
5 **Rights and choices:** human rights, models of development, questioning aid, working for change.
This series has been developed in collaboration with people from the South and offers clearly presented material for investigating the issues.

Views from Brazil
Introducing development issues
DEC (Birmingham) 1990
Profiles of six Brazilians in different occupations and situations, with ideas for discussion and activities.

Where we live
Exploring local–global environment
DEC (Birmingham) and WWF 1992
A textbook for pupils about what is happening to the world environment. Using activities and case studies, links are made between local and global concerns. Development issues and sustainable development are explored throughout.

Ayida
Change and development in Nigeria
Oxfam 1995
Materials for learning about development issues, using a case study of a Nigerian village. Clearly presented activities for exploring different views on change and progress.

Beyond the backyard
Photographs, resources and ideas for a wider understanding of economic realities
DEC (Birmingham) 1993
Support for the inclusion of justice and global interdependence when studying economic awareness. Conceptual ideas about economic activity are made accessible by lively activities, games and people's personal stories. Economic activity from around the world is illustrated in the photographs.

Can you be different?
Resources for understanding internationalisation and cultural change in communities
DEC (Birmingham) 1994
Taiwan is the focus of this pack, which is about the pressures on countries to Westernise. It looks in detail at two communities and how they are affected by links with other nations and cultures. A teachers' handbook, including activity pages for pupils.

Development Compass Rose consultation pack
DEC (Birmingham) 1995 7-adult
This pack uses the Development Compass Rose as a tool for exploring the relationship between development and environment issues. It suggests practical activities based on the photos to highlight the underlying commonality of local issues and those facing people in different parts of the world.

Doorways
Save the Children 1992
An exploration of global housing issues. The case studies and activities are adaptable for a wide age range.

Fala Favela
A photopack
DEC (Birmingham) and Trocaire 1991
Shantytown life in Brazil is explored in this pack. Based on the community of Vila Prudente, it aims to show not only the hardships of life but also the positive dimensions of hope and struggle.

Hanging by a thread

Trade, debt and cotton in Tanzania
Leeds DEC 1992
An active learning pack exploring international issues of trade and debt, using a case study of cotton growing in a region of Tanzania.

Mangla

A study of change and development in Mirpur, 'Azad' Jammu Kashmir, and Pakistan
South Yorkshire DEC 1995
This pack provides wide-ranging materials for examining aspects of change and development in the area of the Mangla dam, and linking them to experiences in Britain.

Pakistan: Change in the Swat valley

ActionAid 1994
Looks at aspects of change in a traditional farming community and suggests activities which encourage pupils to make comparisons with change in their own area.

Speaking for ourselves, listening to others

Leeds DEC 1996
Information and photos from young people in Nairobi provide fresh source material for pupils investigating an urban locality and comparing it with their own.

The backbone of development

Resources and ideas for understanding the role of women in economic development
DEC (Birmingham) 1994
What work do women do? What issues do they face in economic development? Who has the power and how will things change? These are the central questions asked in this photopack, which focuses on case studies from Nepal and Taiwan.

The final frontier?

Land environment and pastoralism in Kenya
Leeds DEC 1994
Active learning materials offering stimulating ways of exploring issues such as land use and economic development from the perspective of Masai pastoralists.

Tibet — a journey through a changing land

A cross-curricular pack for key stages 3 and 4
Tibet Support Group UK and CEWC 1996
This resource on a little-known country contains photos, comprehensive background information, and activities relevant to the geography curriculum as well as to RE, English and humanities.

Resources published by the Geographical Association

Focus on Castries

St Lucia photopack
Vincent Bunce, Jim Foley, Wendy Morgan and Steve Scoble 1992
This pack demonstrates how to teach a distant locality. Contents include 28 A4 colour photographs, comprehensive background information, activities and key questions.

Geography and IT

Investigating aspects of human geography
NCET/GA 1996
This pack is designed to support teachers looking for new opportunities for integrating IT into their teaching. There are a number of example investigations, four of which are supplied as files in various common formats for Acorn, PC and Apple Macintosh.

Images of Earth

A teacher's guide to remote sensing in geography at key stage 3/GCSE
Michael Barnett, Ashley Kent and Mike Milton (eds) 1995
This pack, comprising a 192-page book, 51 aerial photographs and satellite images, 3 full-colour posters and 2 disks of digital satellite-image data, gives you everything you need to bring remote sensing alive in the classroom.

Kaptalamwa

A village in Kenya
Maureen Weldon 1994
This distant-locality study includes numerous maps and photographs, information about the villagers and their way of life, and activity sheets with a PoS focus.

Ladakh photopack

An activity-based pack focused on the life of a Tibetan community
Jo Hughes, Keith Paterson and Paul Rafferty 1992
This pack is based on the life and activities of those living in the settlement of Choglamsar in Ladakh, northern India, and in particular the children attending the Tibetan Children's Village School. It includes 28 A4 colour photographs.

Localities in Malawi

Des Bowden and James Trill 1995

A study of three contrasting localities within Malawi: a traditional rural village, a modern city and an older municipality. The pack includes 29 A4 colour photographs, detailed information, worksheets and key questions.

Montreuil

A European place study
Don Garman (ed) 1995

Developed by a team of primary teachers, this pack offers an in-depth investigation of Montreuil. There are numerous photographs, maps, activity sheets, resource sheets and other material, enabling pupils to 'explore' Montreuil and make comparisons with other localities.

Simulations

The NC and the world beyond

South Yorkshire DEC

Information on eight simulation games which may be purchased separately.

The trading game

Christian Aid 1982

A simulation game illustrating how the world trading system affects the development of countries unequally.

Videos

Action Video Packs

International Broadcasting Trust Production

Developing images

Considers the image presented of the Third World by the media.

Food

Provides a discussion of global food links through a number of case studies.

Energy

Offers a series of case studies relating to the impact of energy consumption.

Rainforests

A discussion of the reasons for, and the effects of, forest exploitation.

The four packs in this series each contain a video, teachers' notes and photocopiable pupils' sheets. They have been designed to provide the pupils with an active role in their learning, encouraging both teacher and pupil to view each short video clip (of between 2 and 5 minutes) as the basic lesson. Suggested activities include stills analysis and storyboarding.

Bangladesh — people and environment

Christian Aid/Team Video 1992

Brazil 2000

BBC 1996

Four programmes: **1** City: Rio de Janeiro, **2** Farming: Big and small, **3** Work: São Paulo, **4** Resources: Carajas.

Geographical Eye Over Africa

International Broadcasting Trust 1995

The programmes engage students' imagination through case studies of individual families and people: farming in contrasting regions of northern and southern Nigeria, in Lagos, in Zambia and along the Zambesi River.

Teachers' guide and photopack also available.

Geographical Eye Over Asia

International Broadcasting Trust 1996

A video containing six programmes first broadcast on Channel 4 Schools in February 1996. Through individual case studies, the programmes enable students to understand how physical conditions influence human activities and are affected by them.

Study guide and pupils' book also available.

Japan 2000

BBC 1995

Investigates the crucial geographical issues facing this remarkable country in the mid-1990s through helicopter footage which allows students to dwell on the geographical patterns of Japan. The four programmes centre around the key topics of manufacturing, industry and energy sources, as well as moving into the more futuristic and alarming issues confronting Japan as it approaches the year 2000.

Neighbours

The life and times of Yesudas Kemal
ActionAid 1992

A videopack focusing on the life of a boy in a small community near Delhi. Information and activity sheets are provided, giving a positive image of a locality in an economically developing country.

USA 2000

BBC 1995

Four programmes: **1** City on the edge — Los Angeles, **2** Lifeblood of the west, **3** Wheelspin in Motor City — Detroit, **4** Safe havens.

Watching the world

Manchester Development Project

A series of programmes on one videotape:

Investigating images

The core unit and an introduction to analysing images.

News from Nicaragua

An introduction to analysing foreign news coverage.

Aspects of Africa

An exploration of perceptions of Africa.

Picture people

Challenging stereotypes.

Whose news?

An introduction to media control and ownership.

This media project explores the role of the media in creating our images of the world and will increase awareness of the media. It suggests techniques and resources that will provide teachers with many ideas which can be applied to video use.

West Africa

BBC 1991

Five programmes including case studies of families in cities and rural areas: **1** On the edge, **2** The price of cocoa, **3** A tale of two citizens, **4** The tourist trade, **5** Oil in the delta.

Working together

The people of Kanjikolly

ActionAid 1994

A videopack featuring a village in South India and the attempts of its tribal people to improve their lives. Includes activity sheets and discussion ideas.

Zig Zag

BBC

This series of programmes is mainly for key stage 2 humanities subjects.

CD-ROMs

Commonwealth Information database

Commonwealth Institute/GINN

IBM PC and compatibles/Acorn Archimedes

Contains information about the countries of the Commonwealth. Text (large) and 3000 pictures, under four general subject areas: politics, economics, land and people. Includes a country navigation bar. Querying is limited to the teacher's notes. Aimed at pupils aged 8–12.

Countries of the World

Anglia TV

IBM PC and compatibles/Acorn Archimedes

A basic atlas using Bartholomews atlas maps. 85 pictures included. Any Key Plus data files can be linked to the maps, using exact latitude and longitude references or with OS grid references. The maps are provided in Key Plus map format.

Requires Key Plus v2 and Keynote v2 or above.

Discover India

ActionAid

IBM PC and compatibles/Acorn Archimedes

Distant Places Interactive Atlas

AU Enterprises Ltd

IBM PC and compatibles

Contains maps from Bartholomews, data from *Philips Geographical Digest* and hundreds of photographs. The underlying Aegis statistical database allows around 200 thematic areas (including population, economy, development, social, agricultural and commodities) to be queried and displayed. Data is displayed as shaded-area maps or as point data, bar charts or pie charts. It included a selection of case studies on St Lucia, Japan, Tanzania, Peru and the Sahara, with data, pictures, text and sound. The text and photos can be enlarged. Includes suggested activities and worksheets, e.g. a role-play activity for locating a new hotel complex on St Lucia.

Encarta

Microsoft

IBM PC and compatible/Acorn Archimedes/RM Nimbus

A multimedia general encyclopaedia, issued annually. The previous year's edition is often available at modest cost.

Environment Series 1 — Water

Nelson Multimedia/YITM

IBM PC and compatibles/Acorn Archimedes

Contains thousands of images, with maps, text and some video footage from Yorkshire Television. There are two main ways to access the disk: Investigate and Tutorial. In Investigate one can explore aspects of water usage throughout history and 17 individual case studies, including flooding in Bangladesh and the Exxon Valdez tanker disaster. The themes for investigation have six key topics: agriculture, industry, fishing, domestic, recreation and transport which cross-reference with general, political, social, economic, scientific and health areas. Searching is largely limited to selected topics. A Trail Save utility is provided to save interesting pages.

Environment Series 2 — Land and Air
Nelson Multimedia/YITM
IBM PC and compatibles/Acorn Archimedes
Contains images, text, and video footage from archives at Yorkshire Television. Subjects covered are dwindling resources, climate change, conservation, natural disasters, food or famine, and air quality. The first three are available as CD-ROM mini-disks. Each subject covered can be searched or explored through a general overview, historical, social and political issues, disadvantages, and an unusual action section which provides ideas for individuals to take further action themselves. There is an interactive overview section which explains the content of the disk. A video sequence introduces each sub-section. Items can be searched using a clear subject-filter index or keywords. Text and pictures can be enlarged, and 'hot words' can be selected for explanation. A Trail Save utility is provided to save the route. Includes photocopiable support sheets.

Kenya: the final frontier
Matrix Multimedia
IBM PC and compatibles

Our World — Volume 1
The Green PC Company Ltd
IBM PC and compatibles
A collection of data covering environmental, political, economic and demographic topics. Data is provided in time-lines, e.g. surface temperatures for the last 200 years, atmospheric CFCs 1931 to the present. It uses a hypertext format and contains summative data for 16 countries only. Each page can be sent to a printer, and up to three graphs can be selected and printed onto one A4 sheet.

People and Places: SCAMP-CD v2.1 (1991)
Pebbleshore
IBM PC and compatibles
Contains 1991 census data from the Office of Population Censuses and Surveys, at all geographical levels from counties to enumeration districts. The data is provided in the form of topic areas, e.g. housing tenure. There are also some derived indicators, such as % moved house and % households with no car. With version 2.1, users select areas and variables by name, rather than numeric codes

as with version 1. The data can be mapped onto digitised boundary maps and also overlaid onto cartographic maps from the Automobile Association. Data can be displayed as shaded-area maps or point data. Subsets of data can be saved for further analysis, for example in a spreadsheet. It is possible to use one's own maps and data with this package.

Physical World
Nelson Multimedia/YITM
IBM PC and compatible/Acorn Archimedes

Small Blue Planet
TAG Developments Ltd/KimTec
IBM PC and compatibles/Apple Macintosh
Contains satellite pictures from NOAA, NASA and LANDSAT of places on the earth at various magnifications. There are four maps or images with a number of hot spots, especially over the USA, which provide access to the satellite images. The political map contains some data on each country, but this is not organised into readily accessible themes. Time zones and day and night can be studied interactively using a 'chronosphere' view, which shows the changing illumination of the earth as viewed from space.

World Atlas v4
Software Tool Works/various distributors, including Koch Media
IBM PC and compatibles/Apple Macintosh
An atlas disk which also contains a useful database with a range of data on government, demographic, economic and environmental factors. These can be displayed globally or by continent, using a simple user interface. Also included is some additional information, such as simple climate graphs, flags and anthems of countries, and some video clips of tourist attractions in the major world cities.

World View
Encyclopaedia Britannica
IBM PC and compatibles/Apple Macintosh
Royalty-free resource disk of 100 photographs and views of the earth from space, with sound clips.

Further reading and references
Books for teachers

75/25, Development in an Increasingly Unequal World Colm Regan (ed) DEC (Birmingham) 1996

Education for Development: a teacher's resource for global learning, Susan Fountain, UNICEF/Hodder and Stoughton 1995

Global Teacher Global Learner, Graham Pike and David Hicks, Hodder and Stoughton 1988

Inside the Third World, Paul Harrison, Penguin 1993

Poverty – answering back, Oxfam/Channel 4 Television 1996

Poverty and the Planet: a question of survival, Ben Jackson, Penguin 1990

Promised Lands: stories of power and poverty in the Third World, Paul Vallelly, Fount/Christian Aid 1992

The Oxfam Poverty Report, Kevin Watkins, Oxfam 1995

The State We're In, Will Hutton, Vintage 1996

Thin Black Lines: Political Cartoons and Development Education, Colm Regan, Scott Sinclair and Martyn Turner, DEC (Birmingham) 1988

Thin Black Lines Rides Again: Political Cartoons and Development Education, Colm Regan, Scott Sinclair and Martyn Turner, DEC (Birmingham) 1994

Voices from ... (Sudan, Uganda etc.), Minority Rights Group 1995

Who are the Street Children? UNICEF 1993

Who Runs the World?, John Madeley, Dee Sullival and Jessica Woodroffe, Christian Aid 1994

Statistical sources

The State of the World's Children, UNICEF, OUP 1995

World Development Report, World Bank, OUP (annual)

Human Development Report, United Nations Development Programme, OUP (annual)

References

Denis Goulet, *Incentives for Development: the key to equity*, New Horizons Press (NY) 1989

The Green Teacher's Resource Book, Green Teacher 1995

The Trading Game, Christian Aid 1993

Rex Walford, 'Games and simulations' in Boardman, D. (ed.) *Handbook for Geography Teachers*, Geographical Association 1986

Paul Webber, 'Agrarian Change in Ghana' in *Geography Review*, vol. 9, no. 3, January 1996

Chris Durbin, 'Geographers on the Internet' in *Teaching Geography,* vol. 21, no. 1, January 1996, pages 15-19

Chris Durbin, 'Using televisual resources in geography' in *Teaching Geography,* vol. 20, no. 3, July 1995, pages 118-121

Focus on Stories, *Severn Trent,* 1995

Useful addresses

Action Aid, Hamlyn House, Archway, London N19 5PG

Advisory Unit for Computers in Education, 126 Great North Road, Hatfield, Herts AL9 5JZ

Anglia TV (SCA), PO Box 18, Benfleet, Essex SS7 1AZ

AU Enterprises Ltd (aka Advisory Unit: Computers in Education)

BBC Educational Publishing, Room 3421, 201 Wood Lane, London W12 3TS

CAFOD, 2 Romero Close, Stockwell Road, London SW9 9TY

Catholic Institute for International Relations, Unit 3, Canonbury Yard, 190a New North Road, Islington, London N1 7BT

Christian Aid, PO Box 100, London SE1 7RT

Commonwealth Institute, Kensington High Street, London W8 6NQ

Development Education Association, Third Floor, 29-31 Cowper Street, London EC2A 4AP

Development Education Centre (Leeds), 153 Cardigan Road, Leeds LS6 1LJ

Development Education Centre (Manchester), c/o Manchester Metropolitan University, 801 Wilmslow Road, Didsbury, Manchester M20 2QR

Development Education Centre (S Yorks), Woodthorpe School, Woodthorpe Road, Sheffield S13 8DD

Encyclopaedia Britannica, Carew House, Station Approach, Wallington, Surrey SM6 0DA

Ginn & Co, Prevendal House, Parson's Fee, Aylesbury, Buckinghamshire HP20 2QZ

Intermediate Technology Development Group, Myson House, Railways Terrace, Rugby CV21 3HT

International Broadcasting Trust, 2 Ferdinand Place, London NW1 8EE

KimTec, 8 Highland Road, Wimborne, Dorset BH21 2QN

Latin American Bureau, 1 Amwell Street, London EC1R 1UL

Matrix Multimedia, 10 Hey Street, Bradford BD7 1DQ

Microsoft call 0345 002000 for your local distributor

NCET, Milburn Hill Road, Science Park, Coventry CV4 7JJ

Nelson Multimedia, Academy Television, 104 Kirkstall Road, Leeds LS3 1JS

Oxfam, 274 Banbury Road, Oxford OX2 7DZ

Pebbleshore Information Services, Lewes Enterprise Centre, 112 Malling Street, Lewes, East Sussex BN7 2RJ

Save the Children Fund, 17 Grove Lane, Camberwell, London SE5 8RD

TAG Development Ltd, 58 Cambell Road, Gravesend, Kent DA11 0JY

The Green PC Company Ltd, PO Box 79, Winchester, Hants SO23 7SD

Third World First, 217 Cowper Street, Oxford OX4 1XG

Tibetan Support Group, 9 Islington Road, London N1 2XH

UNICEF (UK), 55 Lincoln's Inn Fields, London WC24 3NB

Worldaware, 31-35 Kirby Street, London EC1N 8TE

Yorkshire International Thomson Multimedia, Television Centre, 104 Kirkstall Road, Leeds LS3 1JS